# UNVEILED

The Hidden Messages
in the
Parables of Jesus

Festus Eghe Agbonzikilo, PhD.

ISBN 979-8-89345-169-6 (paperback)
ISBN 979-8-89345-170-2 (digital)

Copyright © 2024 by Festus Eghe Agbonzikilo, PhD.

All rights reserved. No part of this publication may be reproduced, distributed, or transmitted in any form or by any means, including photocopying, recording, or other electronic or mechanical methods without the prior written permission of the publisher. For permission requests, solicit the publisher via the address below.

Christian Faith Publishing
832 Park Avenue
Meadville, PA 16335
www.christianfaithpublishing.com

Unless otherwise indicated, all Scripture quotations are taken from the *New International Version (NIV)* of the Bible.

Printed in the United States of America

To my precious Lord and Savior, Jesus Christ, the
eternal One, who is both the message and author
of the message unveiled in this book.
To God the Father, Son, and Holy Spirit, the One who gives
insight into all mysteries and secrets, the One who gives
wisdom to the wise and knowledge to the discerning, the One
who reveals deep and hidden things. The One who knows
what lies in darkness, and light dwells with Him. I'm eternally
grateful for the privilege of your boundless love, grace, and
Holy Spirit. Praise, glory, and honor be to Your holy name!

# CHAPTER 1

# Introduction

The Lord Jesus Christ gave so much information about the kingdom of God and the church during His earthly ministry. This information is encoded and hidden in stories that were told as parables. Parables have two different stories: the surface story and the underlying (hidden) story. While the surface stories of these parables are very relevant and meaningful, for every intent and purpose for which they were told, nevertheless, the underlying message is where the deeper kingdom meaning resides. The Lord Jesus Christ is the only One that could tell such powerful parables with both meaningful surface and underlying messages. One may therefore be tempted to wonder how the Lord Jesus came up with these powerful, meaningful parables. We must remember that the Lord Jesus Christ is the wisdom of God, according to 1 Corinthians 1:24, 30. In Colossians 2:3, we further understand that in Him "dwell all the treasures of wisdom and knowledge." The Lord Jesus is the epitome of wisdom; He's the epitome of knowledge; He's wisdom personified. When the Lord walked the earth, during His earthly ministry, that was wisdom literally having hands and legs and walking the streets of Galilee. The believer, too, has received this wisdom of Christ, for Christ has become for us wisdom from God, righteousness, sanctification, and redemption (1 Corinthians 1:30).

## What is a parable?

- A parable is a mystery, which conveys spiritual secrets (Matthew 13:11, 34–35).
- It is a story used to illustrate a deep, hidden spiritual lesson.
- It is a story within a story, having a surface story and another story hidden underneath, known as the underlying story.
- It is an allegory (Matthew 22:1 TPT—The Passion Translation). It says one thing on the surface but means something else that's much deeper underneath.

## How did the Lord Jesus Christ explain some of His parables?

A parable carries a far deeper message than its literal meaning, as will be seen in the three parables of the Lord Jesus that were privately explained to His disciples.

## The Parable of the Sower

Firstly, the Lord Jesus told the Parable of the Sower and gave the interpretation as something different from the literal meaning (Matthew 13:3–9 and 18–23).

> Then he told them many things in parables, saying: "A farmer went out to sow his seed. As he was scattering the seed, some fell along the path, and the birds came and ate it up. Some fell on rocky places, where it did not have much soil. It sprang up quickly, because the soil was shallow. But when the sun came up, the plants were scorched, and they withered because they had no root. Other seed fell among thorns, which grew up and choked the plants. Still other seed fell on good soil, where it produced a crop—a hundred, sixty or thirty times what was sown." (Matthew 13:3–8)

On the surface, the Parable of the Sower is about a farmer who went about sowing his seed, but in reality, the Lord Jesus wasn't referring to the sowing of seed by any farmer. He meant something far deeper than that, which is the hidden or underlying message conveyed through the parable. This can be seen in the way He explained the parable to His disciples in verses 18–23, as follows:

> Listen then to what the parable of the sower means: When anyone hears the message about the kingdom and does not understand it, the evil one comes and snatches away what was sown in their heart. This is the seed sown along the path. The seed falling on rocky ground refers to someone who hears the word and at once receives it with joy. But since they have no root, they last only a short time. When trouble or persecution comes because of the word, they quickly fall away. The seed falling among the thorns refers to someone who hears the word, but the worries of this life and the deceitfulness of wealth choke the word, making it unfruitful. But the seed falling on good soil refers to someone who hears the word and understands it. This is the one who produces a crop, yielding a hundred, sixty or thirty times what was sown. (Matthew 13:18–23)

Based on the interpretation given by our Lord Jesus Christ, the Parable of the Sower can be broken down into smaller parts to make it much easier to understand:

1. The seed refers to the word of God (message about the kingdom of God).
2. The sowing of the seed by the sower refers to anyone that hears the word of God.
3. The soil where the seed is sown refers to the heart of anyone that hears the word of God.

4. The birds that came to eat up the seed that fell along the path refer to the devil who snatches away what was sown in the heart of that individual. This indicates that the birds in the parable symbolize the devil in reality.
5. The seed falling on rocky ground refers to someone who hears the word and at once receives it with joy. But since they have no root, they last only a short time. When trouble or persecution comes because of the word, they quickly fall away. This shows that the rocky ground symbolizes trouble or persecution.
6. The seed falling among the thorns refers to someone who hears the word, but the worries of this life and the deceitfulness of wealth choke the word, making it unfruitful. This shows that the thorns symbolize the worries of life and the deceitfulness of wealth.
7. The seed falling on good soil refers to someone who hears the word and understands it. This is the one who produces a crop, yielding a hundred, sixty, or thirty times what was sown. This indicates that the good soil symbolizes a good and understanding heart.

## The Parable of the Weeds in the Field

Secondly, the Lord Jesus told the Parable of the Weeds in the Field and gave the interpretation as something different from the literal meaning (Matthew 13:24–30 and 36–43):

> Jesus told them another parable: "The kingdom of heaven is like a man who sowed good seed in his field. But while everyone was sleeping, his enemy came and sowed weeds among the wheat, and went away. When the wheat sprouted and formed heads, then the weeds also appeared. The owner's servants came to him and said, 'Sir, didn't you sow good seed in your field? Where then did the weeds come from?' 'An enemy did this,' he

replied. The servants asked him, 'Do you want us to go and pull them up?' 'No,' he answered, 'because while you are pulling the weeds, you may uproot the wheat with them. Let both grow together until the harvest. At that time I will tell the harvesters: First collect the weeds and tie them in bundles to be burned; then gather the wheat and bring it into my barn.'" (Matthew 13:24–30)

As earlier noted in the Parable of the Sower, the interpretation given by the Lord Jesus isn't the literal meaning of the parable. We see the same thing here in this second parable of the weeds in the field, and the interpretation given by the Lord Jesus is also different from the literal meaning of the parable. The hidden message of the parable can be seen to be far deeper than the literal connotation, as can be seen in the interpretation given in verses 36–39, where the Lord explained the meaning of the parable of the weeds in the field as follows:

> Then he left the crowd and went into the house. His disciples came to him and said, "Explain to us the parable of the weeds in the field." He answered, "The one who sowed the good seed is the Son of Man. The field is the world, and the good seed stands for the people of the kingdom. The weeds are the people of the evil one, and the enemy who sows them is the devil. The harvest is the end of the age, and the harvesters are angels. As the weeds are pulled up and burned in the fire, so it will be at the end of the age. The Son of Man will send out his angels, and they will weed out of his kingdom everything that causes sin and all who do evil. They will throw them into the blazing furnace, where there will be weeping and gnashing of teeth. Then the

righteous will shine like the sun in the kingdom of their Father. Whoever has ears, let them hear." (Matthew 13:36–43)

Based on the interpretation given by our Lord Jesus Christ, the Parable of the Weeds in the Field can be broken down into smaller parts to make it much easier to understand:

1. The one who sowed the good seed represents the Son of Man (our Lord Jesus Christ).
2. The field represents the world.
3. The good seed represents the people of the kingdom (children of God).
4. The weeds represent the people of the evil one (the ungodly).
5. The enemy who sows the weeds represents the devil.
6. The harvest represents the end of the age (the end-time).
7. The harvesters represent the angels.
8. The barn represents the kingdom of God.
9. The burning of the weeds represents the throwing of sinners and evildoers into the blazing furnace, where there will be weeping and gnashing of teeth.

## The Parable of the Net

Thirdly, the Lord told the Parable of the Net and gave the interpretation as something different from the literal meaning (Matthew 13:47–50):

> Once again, the kingdom of heaven is like a net that was let down into the lake and caught all kinds of fish. When it was full, the fishermen pulled it up on the shore. Then they sat down and collected the good fish in baskets, but threw the bad away. This is how it will be at the end of the age. The angels will come and separate the

wicked from the righteous and throw them into the blazing furnace, where there will be weeping and gnashing of teeth.

Based on the interpretation given by our Lord Jesus Christ, the Parable of the Net can be broken down into smaller parts to make it much easier to understand:

1. The fishing represents the end of the age.
2. The fishermen represent angels.
3. The good fish represent righteous people.
4. The bad fish represent wicked people.
5. The basket represents the kingdom of God.
6. The lake where the fishing was done represents the world.
7. The throwing of the bad fish away represents the throwing of the wicked into the blazing furnace, where there will be weeping and gnashing of teeth.

## Important points to note from these three parables

It is very interesting to see the strong relationship between the Parable of the Weeds in the Field and the Parable of the Net. It can be safely concluded that both parables are one and the same, conveying the same underlying message, based on the way both parables were explained by the Lord Jesus Christ. It is vividly clear that some of the characters and events in both parables, although having different names on the surface, represent the same thing in the underlying message. These are highlighted as follows:

1. The field and the lake in both parables represent the world.
2. The harvesters and the fishermen in both parables represent angels.
3. The good seed and the good fish in both parables represent righteous people.
4. The weeds and the bad fish in both parables represent the wicked or ungodly people.

5. The barn and the basket in both parables represent the kingdom of God.
6. The harvest and the fishing in both parables represent the end of the age.
7. The burning of the weeds and the throwing of the bad fish away in both parables represent the throwing of the wicked into the blazing furnace, where there will be weeping and gnashing of teeth.
8. Finally, although the Parable of the Sower has a completely different underlying message from the other two parables, nevertheless, it is important to note that the birds in that parable and the enemy that sows the weeds in the Parable of the Weeds in the Field represent the same person: the devil.
9. It is very insightful to see that two of the three parables explained by the Lord have to do with the end of the age, meaning the parables were given for our generation. We are the end-time generation the Bible spoke about. These parables apply to you and me. I have heard some believers say it's not possible for a loving Father like our God to put anyone in hellfire. But that's not consistent with the words of the Lord Jesus in these two end-time parables that He explained. He stated it categorically, without mincing words, that the wicked and unrighteous people will be thrown into blazing furnace, where there will be weeping and gnashing of teeth. These are the very words of the Lord Jesus Himself. We have a duty to heed these words and walk righteously. This is why He further reiterated this in the book of Revelation, saying, "Don't seal up the words of the prophecy contained in this scroll, because the time is near. Let those who do wrong keep doing what is wrong. Let the filthy still be filthy. Let those who are righteous keep doing what is right. Let those who are holy still be holy. Look! I'm coming soon. My reward is with me, to repay all people as their actions deserve. I am the alpha and the omega, the first and the last, the beginning and the end" (Revelation 22:10–13 CEB—Common English Bible).

10. From these three parables explained by the Lord Jesus, it's explicitly clear that the interpretation of a parable is not the same as its literal meaning. That was exactly how the Lord Jesus treated these parables. He never took them at a surface value. Each parable that was explained by the Lord has a deeper, hidden, underlying kingdom message. The same is true for all other parables that were told by the Lord Jesus Christ, even though He didn't give the underlying interpretation of these other parables to His disciples. We can now depend on the wisdom and insights given by the Holy Spirit to fully understand and comprehend the underlying meaning of these parables.

## Why did the Lord Jesus teach using parables?

It is worth noting that the Lord Jesus spoke these parables to the crowd in the open (Matthew 13:1–3).

> Jesus spoke all these things to the crowd in parables; he did not say anything to them without using a parable. (Matthew 13:34)

However, the interpretations of these parables were only given privately to His disciples. He left the crowd, and His disciples came to Him, asking Him to tell them the meaning of the parable (Matthew 13: 36, 18). The disciples were amazed that the Lord spoke to the crowd in parables. They knew that the parables conveyed deeper messages, but they had no idea what they meant. This is the reason why they came privately to the Lord Jesus to ask Him about the meaning of the parables. They were also concerned that the crowd didn't have a clue about what the Lord Jesus was talking about in the parables (Matthew 13:10).

> The disciples came to him and asked, "Why do you speak to the people in parables?" (Matthew 13:10)

Nevertheless, the Lord gave an interesting answer to their question.

> He replied, "Because the knowledge of the secrets of the kingdom of heaven has been given to you, but not to them." (Matthew 13:11)

From this answer, we understand that the Lord Jesus intentionally spoke to the crowd in parables without giving them the meaning, the reason being that they were not entitled to the meaning of the parables since the parables conveyed the knowledge of the secrets of the kingdom of heaven. He affirmed that this knowledge of kingdom secrets was only given to the disciples, which is the body of Christ today, but not given to those outside the kingdom. It was the disciples alone that had access to the real meaning of these parables, while the crowd went home with the surface stories alone, never knowing what the real, underlying meaning of these parables were. The same is true today. The unveiling of the secrets of the word of God is not to the people of the world but only to the children of God. The mysteries of the kingdom are only given to those that are within—the believers, the children of God—whereas the surface story of the parable is for the crowd. The mysteries of the kingdom have been given to the saints of God. It's our heritage to know these mysteries, for to us it has been given to know these mysteries. It's been freely given to us. This is why the Bible tells us that "now we have received, not the spirit of the world, but the Spirit who is from God, that we might know the things that have been freely given to us by God" (1 Corinthians 2:12 NKJV—New King James Version). These mysteries of the kingdom have been freely made available to us, to know and understand, by the spirit of the Lord. The secrets of God's kingdom are foolishness to the world. This is why the Bible says, "We talk about God's wisdom, which has been hidden as a secret. God determined this wisdom in advance, before time began, for our glory. It is a wisdom that none of the present-day rulers have understood, because if they did understand it, they would never have crucified the Lord of glory!" (1 Corinthians 2:78 CEB). These kingdom secrets are unveiled to us through the spirit of God, according to 1 Corinthians 2:10–11 (CEB), "God has revealed these things to us through the Spirit. The Spirit searches everything, including the depths of God. Who knows a person's depths except their own spirit that lives in them? In the same way, no one has known the depths of God except God's Spirit." Only those in Christ now have access to the secrets of the kingdom. The believer's eyes of understanding have been enlightened (Ephesians 1:18) by the Holy Spirit to understand the things of God. No wonder, the Lord Jesus, before leaving, promised us that He would send another Comforter, the Holy Spirit, to teach us all things and bring to our remembrance the things that He had taught.

> But the Helper, the Holy Spirit, whom the Father will send in My name, He will teach you all things, and bring to your remembrance all things that I said to you. (John 14:26 NKJV)

Now that the Holy Spirit has come, He's teaching us the word of God and reminding us of the things that our Lord Jesus taught us when He walked the earth. For example, the Lord Jesus spoke several parables that were never explained to His disciples privately, possibly because they didn't ask for the interpretation. As a result, we don't have the interpretation of these parables written in the Bible. But since the Holy Spirit has now come, we can depend on Him to open our eyes of understanding and unveil the underlying meaning of these parables to us. That is the purpose of this book: to help the reader understand the hidden messages of some important parables of our Lord Jesus Christ through the help of the Holy Spirit. These parables were left uninterpreted by the Lord as they are hidden messages that are meant for the church that would be born after the Lord's death, resurrection, and ascension to heaven. Unveiling these parables before His gruesome journey to the cross for the salvation of mankind would have left His disciples more confused, needing more questions than answers. Now that the Holy Spirit is here to help and teach us, we can now understand more clearly that the Lord left the believer with powerful messages, which are hidden as parables in the

Gospels. Through the divine help of the Holy Spirit and the insights into mysteries that He provides, some of these parables are discussed in the succeeding chapters of this book to help the believer come to the place of full maturity in Christ, "until we all reach oneness in the faith and in the knowledge of the Son of God, [growing spiritually] to become a mature believer, reaching to the measure of the fullness of Christ [manifesting His spiritual completeness and exercising our spiritual gifts in unity]" (Ephesians 4:13 AMP—Amplified Bible).

## Summary

In this introductory chapter, it has been established that parables are mysteries that convey deep spiritual secrets. It has also been seen that a parable is an allegory, having a surface story and a hidden, underlying message. The Lord Jesus spoke extensively in parables during His earthly ministry. He communicated the deep mysteries of God's kingdom to multitudes using parables, which were often left unexplained to the multitudes. Occasionally, the Lord's disciples privately asked Him to explain His parables to them. This resulted in the Lord explaining the parables of the sower, weeds in the field, and net privately to His disciples, and these three parables have been discussed extensively in this introductory chapter. Ten important points, carefully observed and noted from these parables, have been discussed in this chapter. These three are about the only parables that our Lord Jesus gave the meaning privately to His disciples; for the remaining parables, the disciples didn't ask Him privately for the meaning, so they weren't given. We therefore don't have the privilege of knowing their hidden messages. Since the disciples didn't ask for the meaning, we can now ask the Holy Spirit. Remember, the Lord Jesus promised us that He would ask the Father to send us the Comforter who would teach us all things and bring everything to our remembrance (John 14:26).

> I still have many things to say to you, but you cannot bear them now. However, when He, the Spirit of truth, has come, He will guide

you into all truth; for He will not speak on His own authority, but whatever He hears He will speak; and He will tell you things to come. (John 16:12–13 NKJV)

Now, the Holy Spirit has come, and He's revealing to us the mysteries of the kingdom of God. We can now learn and understand the hidden messages of these parables from the Holy Spirit.

# CHAPTER 2

# The Parable of the Prodigal Son, Also Known as the Parable of the Lost Son (Luke 15:11–32)

Jesus continued: "There was a man who had two sons. The younger one said to his father, 'Father, give me my share of the estate.' So he divided his property between them. Not long after that, the younger son got together all he had, set off for a distant country and there squandered his wealth in wild living. After he had spent everything, there was a severe famine in that whole country, and he began to be in need. So he went and hired himself out to a citizen of that country, who sent him to his fields to feed pigs. He longed to fill his stomach with the pods that the pigs were eating, but no one gave him anything. When he came to his senses, he said, 'How many of my father's hired servants have food to spare, and here I am starving to death! I will set out and go back to my father and say to him: Father, I have sinned against heaven and against you. I am no longer worthy to be called your son; make me like one of your hired servants.' So he got up and went to his father. But while he was still a long way off, his father saw him and was filled with compassion for him; he ran to his son, threw his arms around him and kissed him. The son said to him, 'Father, I have sinned against heaven and against you. I am no longer worthy to be called your son.' But the father said to his servants, 'Quick!

Bring the best robe and put it on him. Put a ring on his finger and sandals on his feet. Bring the fattened calf and kill it. Let's have a feast and celebrate. For this son of mine was dead and is alive again; he was lost and is found.' So they began to celebrate. Meanwhile, the older son was in the field. When he came near the house, he heard music and dancing. So he called one of the servants and asked him what was going on. 'Your brother has come,' he replied, 'and your father has killed the fattened calf because he has him back safe and sound.' The older brother became angry and refused to go in. So his father went out and pleaded with him. But he answered his father, 'Look! All these years I've been slaving for you and never disobeyed your orders. Yet you never gave me even a young goat so I could celebrate with my friends. But when this son of yours who has squandered your property with prostitutes comes home, you kill the fattened calf for him!' My son,' the father said, 'you are always with me, and everything I have is yours. But we had to celebrate and be glad, because this brother of yours was dead and is alive again; he was lost and is found.'"

—Luke 15:11–32

The Parable of the Prodigal Son, also known as the Parable of the Lost Son, is one of the most incredible parables told by our Lord Jesus Christ. It demonstrates the extraordinary love, mercy, and compassion of a gracious father.

## Unveiling the Parable of the Prodigal Son

Let us begin with the characters in the parable.

1. *The father*: The father in this parable symbolizes our Heavenly Father, the Lord God Almighty. Our Father in heaven is a God of great mercy and compassion, as demonstrated by the father in the parable. This is why the Bible says, "But you, Lord, are a compassionate and gracious God, slow to anger, abounding in love and faithfulness"

(Psalm 86:15). Our Heavenly Father is a compassionate and gracious God. He is gracious and righteous in all His ways, the reason the psalmist proclaimed, "The Lord is gracious and righteous; our God is full of compassion" (Psalm 116:5). The father showed extraordinary love and compassion to his erstwhile prodigal son. He received him back home without anger or bitterness. He easily forgave and forgot all his wrongs. He demonstrated his richness in love and compassion to his lost son. This is consistent with the scripture that says, "The Lord is gracious and compassionate, slow to anger and rich in love. The Lord is good to all; he has compassion on all he has made" (Psalm 145:8–9). The psalmist further repeated this, saying, "The Lord is compassionate and gracious, slow to anger, abounding in love" (Psalm 103:8). Moses, the man of God, had a glimpse of this on Mount Sinai when the Lord came down in the cloud, "and he passed in front of Moses, proclaiming, 'The Lord, the Lord, the compassionate and gracious God, slow to anger, abounding in love and faithfulness'" (Exodus 34:6). The compassionate nature of our Heavenly Father is greatly demonstrated in this parable. Our God is good. His goodness extends to all mankind. The psalmist knew this overwhelming goodness of God when he boldly declared, "Oh, that men would give thanks to the Lord for His goodness, and for His wonderful works to the children of men" (Psalm 107:8 NKJV). The Lord's compassion and loving-kindness are unfathomable and indescribable. This is why the prophet Jeremiah proclaimed, "Because of the Lord's great love we are not consumed, for his compassions never fail" (Lamentations 3:22).

2. *The first son*: The first son in this parable symbolizes Israel or Jews. Israel is God's firstborn son, according to the italicized portion of the following scripture, which says, "Then say to Pharaoh, 'This is what the Lord says: *Israel is my firstborn son*,' and I told you, 'Let my son go, so he may worship me.' But you refused to let him go; so I will kill

your firstborn son" (Exodus 4:22–23). The apostle Paul, by the spirit of God, sheds light on this further when he wrote that God's message of salvation to mankind is "first to the Jew," before the rest of the world. The reason is because Israel is God's firstborn son, symbolized by the first son in this parable. This is further shown in the italicized portion of the following scripture that says, "For I am not ashamed of the gospel, because it is the power of God that brings salvation to everyone who believes: *first to the Jew*, then to the Gentile" (Romans 1:16). From these two scriptures, we can see that the firstborn son represents the Jews or children of Israel. They are God's firstborn son. Before the birth of the church of Jesus Christ, the Jews were the only children of God on earth. They were the only people that knew the Almighty God. Abraham was the father of Isaac, who had two sons, Esau and Jacob. God later changed Jacob's name to Israel (Genesis 32:28). Since Israel is the grandson of Abraham, it therefore means that the children of Israel (Jews) are the descendants of Abraham. Following God's covenant with Abraham in Genesis 12:1–3, the descendants of Abraham, the Jews, became the bona fide children of Almighty God. This is why they are regarded as God's firstborn son among the sons of men, symbolized by the first son in this parable.

3. *The prodigal (or lost) son*: The prodigal son symbolizes the Gentiles, which are the people that remain aside the Jews. The whole world minus the Jews, whatever remains, are the Gentiles. The following scriptures give further insight into the identity of the prodigal (or lost) son in the parable, especially the parts that have been italicized: "Is God the God of Jews only? Is he not *the God of Gentiles too*? Yes, of Gentiles too" (Romans 3:29). This is also seen in the earlier scripture that says, "For I am not ashamed of the gospel, because it is the power of God that brings salvation to everyone who believes: first to the Jew, *then to the Gentile*" (Romans 1:16). The Jews are the first son,

while the Gentiles are the second son. Before the church of Christ was born, the children of Israel were the only people on earth that served the Almighty God as their God. Like the dedicated first son in the parable, the children of Israel were dedicated to serving God as the God of their fathers and nation. This wasn't the case with the younger brother, the prodigal son, which symbolizes the Gentiles, who abandoned God, their Creator, and went into idolatry and paganism. But because of the finished work of Christ for mankind on the cross, the Gentiles have been brought back into the family of God. The Gentiles are now part of the commonwealth of God. This is the underlying message of this parable; it's the return of the Gentiles from their idolatry and paganism back to God Almighty, their Creator. The parable is about the divine plan of God for the salvation of all mankind, especially the return of the Gentiles to the family of God through Christ our Lord.

So far, the following have already been established:

1. The father symbolizes our Heavenly Father, God Almighty.
2. The first son symbolizes Israel.
3. The prodigal son symbolizes the Gentiles.

## Important points to note from the Parable of the Prodigal Son

1. *The prodigal son hired himself out to a citizen of that country, who sent him to his fields to feed pigs* (vs 15–16): This symbolizes the deadly, disgraceful, and shameful nature of sin. This is the level sin can bring a man to. Sin brings a man to his knees and lowest ebb, the reason the scripture says, "The soul that sins, it shall die" (Ezekiel 18:20), which is further corroborated in the New Testament in Romans 3:23, which says, "For the wages of sin is death." Sin is deadly. Never flirt with sin. Flee from it by every possible means. Sin brings shame and reproach to a man's life.

This is why Proverbs 14:34 (NKJV) says, "Righteousness exalts a nation, But sin is a reproach to any people." Looking at the context of this parable, the Jews don't eat pig; it's regarded as unclean. But sin brought the prodigal son to the level where he longed to eat the food being served to pigs. This is the level sin can bring a man to. Sin brings man to the lowest level. Sin brings a man to his knees. You will never long to eat the food being served to pigs. Sin will not be pleasant to you. It will not have dominion over you. This is how the Gentiles were before Christ brought salvation to mankind; they longed to eat the food of pigs. The Gentiles were wasteful, prodigal, and frivolous. They wasted and squandered their lives in idolatry and paganism, like the prodigal son. The apostle Paul, by the spirit of God, alluded to this when He said the Gentiles were led and carried away to dumb idols.

> You know that you were Gentiles, carried away to these dumb idols, however you were led. (1 Corinthians 12:2 NKJV)

When God blessed them with good things, such as children, rainfall, bountiful harvest in their farms, they would ascribe these good things to their idols, supposing that it was their idols and gods that gave them those good things. We see this play out in the experience of the apostles, Paul and Barnabas, in Lystra, a Gentile nation:

> In Lystra there sat a man who was lame. He had been that way from birth and had never walked. He listened to Paul as he was speaking. Paul looked directly at him, saw that he had faith to be healed and called out, "Stand up on your feet!" At that, the man jumped up and began to walk. When the crowd saw what Paul had done, they shouted in the Lycaonian language, "The gods have come down to us in human form!" Barnabas they called Zeus, and Paul they called

Hermes because he was the chief speaker. The priest of Zeus, whose temple was just outside the city, brought bulls and wreaths to the city gates because he and the crowd wanted to offer sacrifices to them. But when the apostles Barnabas and Paul heard of this, they tore their clothes and rushed out into the crowd, shouting: "Friends, why are you doing this? We too are only human, like you. We are bringing you good news, telling you to turn from these worthless things to the living God, who made the heavens and the earth and the sea and everything in them. In the past, he let all nations go their own way. Yet he has not left himself without testimony: He has shown kindness by giving you rain from heaven and crops in their seasons; he provides you with plenty of food and fills your hearts with joy." Even with these words, they had difficulty keeping the crowd from sacrificing to them. (Acts 14:8–18)

These Lystra Gentiles were so rife in idolatry, and the same is still true for many Gentiles around the world today. Had the apostles not stopped them, they would have sacrificed to them, having concluded that they were gods. That was easy for them to do because it's natural to them; it's their way, the way of idolatry. They turned the apostles Barnabas and Paul to gods. The Lystra Gentiles got the blessing of a great miracle from God Almighty, resulting in the complete healing of a lame man. Instead of giving praises and thanks to God, they decided it was the "gods" who gave them that miracle. The Gentiles squandered their God-given blessings in idolatry. That was like the prodigal son, who squandered his portion of wealth inherited from his father in riotous, wasteful living. Idolatry and paganism by the Gentiles brought them into deep spiritual poverty, sin, and lack, to the point of being in deep need, wanting to eat from the food being served to pigs. This sadly remains the story today of anyone who's not in Christ Jesus, whether Jew or Gentile. However, if that individual repents and accepts Christ as his Lord and Savior, he will receive the right to become a child of the living God, according to John 1:12, which says, "Yet to all who did receive him, to those who believed in his name, he gave the right to become children of God."

2. *The prodigal son came to his senses and returned home to his father* (vs 17–21): This symbolizes repentance. Repentance means turning away from sin and returning to God. When we repent of our sins and return to God, He will accept us. Repentance is a personal choice and decision. God will never compel anyone to repent. The prodigal son came to his senses and decided he had had enough of starvation and the crave to eat foods being fed to pigs. He decided, on his own volition, to take that bold step to return home to his father. It was his decision. It was his choice. He called that shot, having come to his senses. Had he not made that choice or decision, he wouldn't have known that his father was waiting with open arms to receive him back to the family. This is the power of repentance. It's our duty to repent; it's God's mercy to forgive and accept us back. It's worth stating that God always has His arms wide open to receive any prodigal son or daughter back home. The prodigal son was still on the way, far away from home, when his father ran toward him to receive him back. In verses 21–22, "the son said to him, 'Father, I have sinned against heaven and against you. I am no longer worthy to be called your son.' But the father said to his servants, 'Quick! Bring the best robe and put it on him. Put a ring on his finger and sandals on his feet.'" While he was still on the way, the father received him. The father ran to him. The father never responded to his apologies because the father never remembered the wrong that the son did. Repentance is turning away from evil. God is more interested in you making a U-turn than telling Him "I'm sorry"; all you need do is to turn away from that thing. The best robe means there are at least three types of robes. The father didn't say, "Give him the good robe or the better robe," instead, he was given the best robe. The father gave him the best robe for choosing to return home (repentance). The fact that

the father sighted the son far away and ran toward him implies that there were days that the father stared in the distance, hoping perhaps the lost son would be on his way back home. The father was expectant that this lost son would return to his senses and return home someday. He was on the lookout for his lost son. God is always on the lookout for unbelieving sons and daughters to repent and return home. He is "not wanting anyone to perish, but everyone to come to repentance" (2 Peter 3:9). The Lord is willing and ready to forgive anyone that repents, no matter how great the sin may be. The reason His word says, "'Come now, let us settle the matter,' says the Lord. 'Though your sins are like scarlet, they shall be as white as snow; though they are red as crimson, they shall be like wool'" (Isaiah 1:18). The Lord Jesus demonstrated this character of the Father when He declared, "Whoever comes to me I will never drive away" (John 6:37). No matter how deep a man is in the pit of sin, when he turns to the Lord Jesus, He said He would never drive him away. What a God of mercy, love, and compassion! The Lord Jesus Christ is full of grace and truth (John 1:16). He's the epitome of grace and truth personified. His grace is sufficiently abundant to forgive any sinner that would choose to repent and return home.

> But where sin abounded, grace abounded much more. (Romans 5:20 NKJV)

Repentance is the very first step to salvation, as clearly shown in the Salvation Flow Chart in figure 1. Without repentance, there can never be salvation. The Lord is "not willing that any should perish but that all should come to repentance" (2 Peter 3:9 NKJV). The time of this ignorance is past. Now, God is calling all men to repentance.

> In the past God overlooked such ignorance, but now he commands all people everywhere to repent. For he has set a day when he will judge the world with justice by the man he has appointed.

> He has given proof of this to everyone by raising him from the dead. (Acts 17:30–31)

3. *The father hugged and kissed the prodigal son* (vs 20–21): This symbolizes forgiveness. When we return to God, we receive the forgiveness of sin. When people reconcile, they hug and kiss, meaning they have put their differences aside and made a truce of peace. This is why the Bible says, "Therefore, since we have been justified through faith, we have peace with God through our Lord Jesus Christ" (Romans 5:1). The prodigal son received the remission of sins, the complete obliteration (removal) of sin, according to Matthew 26:28 and Acts 2:38. The father remembers his sin no more, as stated in Hebrews 8:12, saying, "For I will forgive their wickedness and will remember their sins no more." Hebrews 10:17 further repeats this, saying, "Then he adds: 'Their sins and lawless acts I will remember no more.'" Although the Greek word translated as "forgiveness," and remission is from the same word *aphesis*, but both forgiveness and remission are not the same. Remission is far greater than forgiveness, and that's what we have received in Christ Jesus. The remission of sin has to do with the blotting out, obliteration, or total removal of sin, as clearly expressed in Isaiah 43:25, which says, "I, even I, am he who blots out your transgressions, for my own sake, and remembers your sins no more." The prodigal son received the remission of sin, the father blotting out his sin and remembering them no more, leading to justification and peace with God (Romans 5:1). The remission of sin makes justification possible, which acquits a sinner of the charges against him, declaring him not guilty in the process. The prodigal son was still on his way when the father received and kissed him. The father, twice, didn't respond to the son's plea for forgiveness because his decision to return home (by receiving Christ) is the act of repentance. This agrees with the scripture in Romans 5:8, which says, "But God demonstrates His own love toward us, in that while we were still sinners, Christ died for us."

4. *The prodigal son is given the best robe*: "But the father said to his servants, 'Quick! Bring the best robe and put it on him'" (vs 22). The best robe symbolizes God's righteousness and eternal life. This can be seen in the scripture, which says, "Everything I did was honest. *Righteousness covered me like a robe*, and I wore justice like a turban" (Job 29:14 NLT—New Living Translation). The prophet Isaiah made a similar proclamation, when he said, "I will greatly rejoice in the Lord, my soul shall be joyful in my God; for He has clothed me with the garments of salvation, *He has covered me with the robe of righteousness*" (Isaiah 61:10 NKJV). That is exactly what the prodigal son received from his father; he received righteousness from the father in the form of a robe. This is also found in the New Testament, the book of Revelation, where it says, "And to her was granted that she should be arrayed in fine linen, clean and white: *for the fine linen is the righteousness of saints*" (Revelation 19:8 KJV—King James Version). From this scripture in Revelation, we understand that this robe is made of fine linen, representing the righteousness of saints. This is the same robe that the prodigal son received from his father; it's the righteousness of saints. Righteousness means right standing with God, a state of moral and spiritual rightness with God, absolved of every guilt and blame, on account of faith in the finished work of Christ on the cross. The foundation upon which the righteousness of God is established for the believer is justification, which means "to be declared not guilty." Following the hug and kiss given to the prodigal son by the father, symbolizing the remission of his sins, the son is therefore justified and declared not guilty. On this basis, he's imputed or credited with the gift of righteousness, which the best robe symbolizes. This is how Romans 5:1 put it: "Therefore, since we have been justified through faith, we have peace with God through our Lord Jesus Christ." Justification opens the door wide for mankind to receive the righteousness of God in Christ Jesus, which is a gift according to Romans 5:17, "For if, by the trespass of the one man, death reigned through that one man, how much more will those who receive God's abundant provision of grace

and of *the gift of righteousness* reign in life through the one man, Jesus Christ!" The righteousness of God goes together with the life of God. When anyone receives the righteousness of God, which is in Christ Jesus, the divine life of God, also known as *zoe* (Greek), is freely made available to that individual. The robe represents God's type of life. The best robe is what has been given to those who believe in the Lord Jesus Christ, which is the church or body of Christ. The church of Christ is the best and greatest creation of God. The "best robe" implies that there are at least three different types of robes of righteousness. Four types of robes are given as follows, in the order of their superiority. The most superior robe is the one listed in item d, which is the same as the "best robe":

a. *The robe of sin and self-righteousness*: This is the robe of sin, carrying the righteousness of the fallen nature of man. This is self-righteousness, which is like a filthy rag before God. This is what the Bible says about this type of robe of righteousness:

> We are all infected and impure with sin. When we put on our prized robes of righteousness, we find they are but filthy rags. Like autumn leaves we fade, wither, and fall. And our sins, like the wind, sweep us away. (Isaiah 64:6 TLB—The Living Bible)

This is exemplified in scripture when Joshua the high priest stood before an angel of the Lord:

> Now Joshua was dressed in filthy clothes as he stood before the angel. The angel said to those who were standing before him, "Take off his filthy clothes." Then he said to Joshua, "See, I have taken away your sin, and I will put fine garments on you." (Zechariah 3:3–4)

The robe of sin and self-righteousness is what Adam passed down to all mankind. Every human being that's born into this world comes with the fallen nature of sin from Adam, which is passed on to every man as the robe of sin and self-righteousness. This robe falls short of God's standard and glory, according to Romans 3:23, which says, "For all have sinned and fall short of the glory of God." So this is the first type of robe; it's also the worst type of robe. It represents sin and the fallen Adamic nature.

b. *The robe of righteousness by the law* (Romans 10:5; Romans 3:20): This is the righteousness that comes from the law of Moses. The law could not give life (Galatians 3:21). The law could not make anything perfect (Hebrews 7:19). This was the righteousness of everyone that lived under the law. This is the same righteousness that the Pharisees had during the earthly ministry of the Lord Jesus. The righteousness of the law is imperfect; the reason the Lord Jesus said, "For I tell you that unless your righteousness surpasses that of the Pharisees and the teachers of the law, you will certainly not enter the kingdom of heaven" (Matthew 5:20). The Pharisees and the teachers of the law had this imperfect righteousness.

c. *The robe of righteousness by faith* (Romans 10:6): This is the righteousness of the patriarchs who walked faithfully with God before the law of Moses ever existed. For example, Enoch, Noah, Abraham, Isaac, Jacob, etc. served God faithfully and were made righteous because of their faithful walk with God. These patriarchs believed God, walking by faith, and were credited with the righteousness of God by faith (Genesis 15:6; Romans 4:3; and Galatians 3:6). This righteousness is not the same as the righteousness of God through faith in Jesus Christ. That's only possible to those who have received Christ as their Lord and Savior, the one that's born again, which is the church today. The patriarchs were not born again during their earthly walk, as they lived before Christ was born. Therefore, it was not possible for them to have the righteousness of God through faith in Jesus Christ. The robe of righteousness by faith is superior to the robes of self-righteousness and the law but inferior to the best robe, which is the robe of righteousness of God through faith in Jesus Christ. That's the highest form of righteousness because it's God's own type of righteousness.

d. *The robe of righteousness of God through faith in Jesus Christ* (Romans 3:22; 2 Corinthians 5:21; and Galatians 2:16): This is the righteousness that's given as a gift to anyone who believes in Jesus Christ. It's the righteousness of God Himself, which is given as a gift and imputed (credited) to the believer through faith in Jesus Christ and His finished work for mankind on the cross. This is the best and greatest type of righteousness, superior to all others, the reason it's called the best robe, meaning it's the best righteousness there is. It's only found and available in Christ. No human work can attain to this standard of righteousness. It cannot be earned. It cannot be bought. It's only given as a gift to those who have received Christ. The adjective *best* has been used to qualify this robe. This happens when three or more items are being compared. If only two items are being compared, then *good* and *better* are used. However, if there are three or more items, then it becomes *good*, *better*, and *best*. In this case, we have seen four different types of robes, and the fourth one is the best robe, signifying supremacy over the others. The word *best* means the finest, the greatest, the topmost, the supreme, the foremost. All these words accurately qualify the righteousness of God through faith in Jesus Christ. This is the best type of righteousness. It's the finest, greatest, topmost, foremost, and supreme type of righteousness. It's the ultimate and perfect righteousness. It's God's own standard of righteousness given to those who believe in Jesus Christ. Interestingly, this has now become the only acceptable type of righteousness to God. This is the reason God wants all men to come to Jesus Christ so that they can receive this righteousness and be pleasing to

God. This righteousness does not exist outside Christ. It's only found in Christ. This is the chief reason why Christ is the only way for mankind to reconnect to God. While responding to the question Thomas asked about how they would know the way to God, the Lord Jesus said to him, "I am the way, the truth, and the life. No one comes to the Father except through Me" (John 14:6). This righteousness is only available in Christ, the reason Christ is the only way to God.

The first son in the parable, symbolizing Israel, is wearing the second type of robe, which is the robe of righteousness of the law of Moses. This is the same robe that the Pharisees wore during the earthly ministry of our Lord Jesus Christ, and it's the same robe that the Jews wore until the law was abrogated when the Lord Jesus Christ died on the cross of Calvary. Following His death on the cross, the law and the prophets were fulfilled in Christ, and the law was therefore abrogated (Ephesians 2:14–15). Consequently, the righteousness of the law has now ceased to exist. In the same vein, following Christ's work of salvation on the cross, for all mankind, the righteousness of faith has also ceased to exist. There are no more intermediary grounds for righteousness. A man is either having the righteousness of Christ or self-righteousness with the fallen Adamic nature of sin. Therefore, the only type of righteousness that's available and acceptable to God today, for all mankind, is the righteousness of God through faith in Jesus Christ. This is the believer's robe, which is the best robe. The believer's robe is the ultimate righteousness. It brings him into fellowship with God the Father, Son, and Spirit, and this fellowship is the believer's highest calling. The reason why we are the children of God is so we may be in continuous fellowship with our Father, according to 1 John 1:1–3 and 2 Corinthians 13:14. The best robe in this parable is very powerful. It's the first gift that the prodigal son received from his father. All other gifts that followed thereafter—the ring, shoes, and celebration feast—came because the son had already received the ultimate gift of the best robe. There is so much revelation in this best robe to still unpack. This is further discussed in-depth in a separate section at the end of this chapter, where the best robe is seen to be a great gift and a great mystery.

5. *The prodigal son is given a ring*: "Put a ring on his finger..." (vs 22). The ring given to the prodigal son symbolizes our Christ-given power and authority, which combine to produce dominion. Having successfully unveiled the dreams of Pharoah, Joseph was given dominion and put in charge of the whole land of Egypt through the ring that Pharoah gave to him:

> So Pharaoh said to Joseph, "I hereby put you in charge of the whole land of Egypt." *Then Pharaoh took his signet ring from his finger and put it on Joseph's finger...* (Genesis 41:41–42)

The signet ring given to Joseph put him in charge of Egypt, giving him power, authority, and dominion. The same is true for the believer who has dominion in Christ. The believer's dominion is derived from two sources:

   a. *The power of the Holy Spirit*: The believer receives his Christ-given power from the Holy Spirit. This is why the scripture says, "But you will receive power when the Holy Spirit comes on you; and you will be my witnesses in Jerusalem, and in all Judea and Samaria, and to the ends of the earth" (Acts 1:8). The word *power* in this scripture is from the Greek word *dunamis*, from which words like *dynamite, dynamo,* and *dynamics* are derived. The power of the Holy Spirit is the same power that God used in raising Christ from the dead (Romans 8:11). This is the same power that is at work in the life of the believer. During the earthly ministry of the Lord Jesus Christ, it was this same power that was at work in Him, by which He went about doing good and healing all that were oppressed of the devil, according to Acts 10:38, which says, "How God anointed Jesus of Nazareth with the Holy Spirit and power, and how he went around doing good and healing all who were under the power of the devil, because God was with him." The Holy Spirit and power go together. He's the power behind the creation of God. He's also the power behind the supernatural works of God. Through the Holy Ghost, the believer has access to the limitless power of God Almighty.

b. *The authority in the name of Jesus*: While the believer's power comes from the Holy Spirit, however his authority is in the name of Jesus Christ. Just as the Holy Spirit and power go together, that's how the name of Jesus Christ and authority go together. The believer has been given the power of attorney to use the name of Jesus Christ. By this, he can exercise tremendous authority through the name of Jesus. God has highly exalted the Lord Jesus Christ to the highest place and given Him a name that's above all names, according to Philippians 2:9–11, which says, "Therefore God exalted him to the highest place and gave him the name that is above every name, that at the name of Jesus every knee should bow, in heaven and on earth and under the earth, and every tongue acknowledge that Jesus Christ is Lord, to the glory of God the Father." The name of the Lord Jesus Christ is the greatest and most powerful name in the universe. This name carries all power and authority. This is the name that has been given to us, the believers. In Mark 16:17–18, the Lord Jesus assured us that "these signs will accompany those who believe: In my name they will drive out demons; they will speak in new tongues; they will pick up snakes with their hands; and when they drink deadly poison, it will not hurt them at all; they will place their hands on sick people, and they will get well." Believers have been empowered, through the name of Jesus, to drive out demons. You would observe that driving out demons is the first thing on the list; that is because it's our heritage and honor to drive out demons. Every believer in Christ has been given the authority and power to drive out demons. This is done by exercising the power of attorney that is in the name of Jesus Christ. In Luke 10:17–19, we see an interesting account, when the Lord Jesus sent out the seventy-two to go out and preach about the kingdom:

> The seventy-two returned with joy and said, "Lord, even the demons submit to us in your name." He replied, "I saw Satan fall like lightning from heaven. I have given you authority to trample on snakes and scorpions and to overcome all the power of the enemy; nothing will harm you."

As seen in this scripture, demons submit at the mention of the name of Jesus. I particularly love the phrase that says, "I have given you authority to trample…" The word *authority* here is from the Greek word *exousia*.

The combination of both *exousia* (authority) and *dunamis* (power) gives the believer incredible dominion in Christ Jesus. We have been given the power of attorney of the name of Jesus Christ. With that name, we conquer everything and anything. Everything we say or do must be done in the name of our Lord Jesus Christ (Colossians 3:17). Never trivialize the name of Jesus. It is the greatest name in the universe. We have the Holy Spirit divine who empowers us. The reason for the mighty power that was demonstrated by the Lord Jesus during His earthly ministry is because of the Holy Ghost anointing He received (Acts 10:38 and Luke 4:1, 18). The Lord has empowered us by His name and Holy Spirit. To maximize the manifestation of our dominion in Christ, we must walk closely with the Holy Spirit daily. Secondly, we must abide daily in the word of the living God. In response to the Sadducees, "Jesus replied, 'You are in error because you do not know the Scriptures or the power of God'" (Matthew 22:29). Without the correct and accurate knowledge of God's word, the believer would be in error. There would be incongruity between the dominion Christ has given to him and the reality on the ground. The accurate knowledge of God's word, with understanding, is vital for a believer to maximally exercise the power and authority that have been received in Christ. The Christian life is a life of faith. The Christ-given power and authority are manifested by faith. The believer must ensure therefore to feed continuously on the living word of God, for the word of God is the food of faith.

> So then faith comes by hearing, and hearing by the word of God. (Romans 10:17 NKJV)

6. *Shoes on his feet*: "…and sandals on his feet" (vs 22). The shoes given to the prodigal son symbolize the Great Commission, our Christ-given mandate to proclaim the good news of salvation to all men. The apostle Paul, by the spirit of God, knew this when he said, "And put *shoes on your feet* so that you are ready *to spread the good news of peace*" (Ephesians 6:15 CEB). Similarly, the prophet Isaiah, also by the same spirit of God, saw this prophetically and declared, "How beautiful on the mountains are *the feet of those who bring good news*, who proclaim peace, who bring good tidings, who proclaim salvation, who say to Zion, 'Your God reigns!'" (Isaiah 52:7). The gospel of Jesus Christ is good news. It's the good news of peace, glad tidings, and salvation to all mankind, the reason why the angel and a multitude of the heavenly host rejoiced and praised God when Christ was born, saying, "Glory to God in the highest, and on earth peace, goodwill toward men!" (Luke 2:14 NKJV). The shoes on the feet symbolize the mandate given to the believer to go tell the untold that salvation has come for all mankind. Life has come; there is no more death. Light has come; there is no more darkness. Redemption has come; there is no more condemnation. Righteousness has come; there is no more sin. Christ has come to give abundant life to man. This is the good news of the gospel: the salvation of mankind by Jesus Christ. The shoes on the feet represent the commitment of the gospel of Jesus Christ to the believer. The earlier scripture in Isaiah was quoted by the apostle Paul in Romans 10:15, saying, "And how can anyone preach unless they are sent? As it is written: 'How beautiful are the feet of those who bring good news!'" The one who is

in Christ has been sent to preach the gospel. The believer has been mandated to be a witness for Christ. He's to go into the world and be Christ's witness and ambassador (2 Corinthians 5:18–20), reconciling the world back to God, who has reconciled us to himself through Christ and gave us the ministry of reconciliation, committing to us the message of reconciliation (2 Corinthians 5:18–19).

## Three important points to note about the shoes on the feet:

a. *It is mandatory to wear these shoes on your feet*: The believer is mandated to proclaim the gospel of Christ. This is a command, not a suggestion. The apostle Paul highlighted the importance of this command when he said he was compelled to preach the gospel. For him, preaching the good news was not something negotiable. It was the very essence of his living. He felt compelled to always witness for Christ. In fact, he went as far as laying a curse (woe) on himself if he preached not the gospel. That is how prepared he was to tell the untold about the good news of Jesus Christ:

> For when I preach the gospel, I cannot boast, since I am compelled to preach. Woe to me if I do not preach the gospel! (1 Corinthians 9:16)

This shows the severity of this mandate and the urgent need to fulfill it. All believers must be involved in spreading the good news of Jesus Christ to a hurting world. The harvest, truly, is ripe, but the workers are few. Therefore to fulfill this great task, all hands must be on deck. The believer must yield to this call and be the answer to the prayer for the Lord of the harvest to send more workers to His harvest field. The Lord Jesus said to the seventy-two, "The harvest is plentiful, but the workers are few. Ask the Lord of the harvest, therefore, to send out workers into his harvest field" (Luke 10:2).

The Great Commission is a clarion call for the believer to step out in faith as a worker in the Lord's harvest field.

> b. *You have been empowered to wear these shoes on your feet*: The believer has not been tasked with fulfilling this Great Commission in his own power and ability. The empowerment of the Holy Spirit has been given for this mandate. From scriptures, we understand that the believer must receive the Holy Spirit and power, in the first instance, before stepping out in faith to witness for Christ:
>
>> But you will receive power when the Holy Spirit comes on you; and you will be my witnesses in Jerusalem, and in all Judea and Samaria, and to the ends of the earth. (Acts 1:8)

The empowerment by the Holy Spirit is a prerequisite for the fulfillment of this mandate. The Lord Jesus did not permit the apostles to preach the gospel until they were endued with the Holy Ghost. That is what we have just read in Acts 1:8, where the first statement, "but you will receive power when the Holy Spirit comes on you," is the empowerment, while the second statement, "and you will be my witnesses in Jerusalem, and in all Judea and Samaria, and to the ends of the earth," is the Great Commission. The empowerment by the Holy Ghost must always precede the assignment to witness for Christ. This is very important. The same happened in the life of the Lord Jesus Himself during His earthly ministry. He did not go about preaching the good news of the kingdom until He was anointed with the Holy Ghost and power, according to the prophecy of Isaiah (Isaiah 61:1), which the Lord Jesus read out to the hearing of the people in the temple in Luke 4:18–19, saying, "The Spirit of the Lord is on me, because he has anointed me to proclaim good news to the poor. He has sent me to proclaim freedom for the prisoners and recovery of sight for the blind, to set the oppressed free, to proclaim the year of the Lord's favor." Similarly, the Lord had to be anointed with the Holy Ghost and power before going about doing good, healing all that were oppressed of the devil (Acts 10:38), proclaiming the good news of the kingdom. Acts 1:8 shows that the *ring* (power of the Holy Spirit) must be given before the *shoes on the feet* (the mandate to preach the gospel). Putting the shoes on the feet before giving out the ring is like putting the cart before the horse. That won't work. You must be empowered before heading out to preach the gospel. The prodigal son was first given the ring before the shoes. That means we must first be empowered by the Holy Spirit before going into the world to preach the gospel to others. That is exactly what the Lord Jesus instructed His disciples in Acts 1:8. The disciples tarried in Jerusalem until they were first endued with the power of the Holy Spirit before going out to preach the gospel.

   c. *There is great reward for you to wear these shoes on your feet*: The Great Commission is God's ministry of reconciliation. So it is God's big business here on earth. There are both earthly and eternal rewards for those who heed this call. Daniel 12:3 says, "Those who are wise will shine like the brightness of the heavens, and those who lead many to righteousness, like the stars for ever and ever." If you partner with God and lead many to righteousness, the scripture assures that you would shine like the stars forever and ever. This eternal reward is of immense value. The apostle Paul sheds further light on this when he said, "If I preach voluntarily, I have a reward; if not voluntarily, I am simply discharging the trust committed to me. What then is my reward? Just this: that in preaching the gospel I may offer it free of charge, and so not make full use of my rights as a preacher of the gospel" (1 Corinthians 9:17–18).

The gospel has been committed to our care. God wants us to preach the gospel everywhere. The shoe is not for partying; it is for proclaiming the gospel to the whole world. The power of the kingdom is manifested on the go in the marketplace, where we proclaim this good news to the world. God wants us to bring souls to the kingdom. When you stand before the Lord Jesus, what are you going to show to Him as your harvest of souls? What excuses are you going to give for not witnessing for Him? Would you say to Him that you've been extremely busy with your job or looking after your family, business, or ministry? We must go about our Father's business, the same way our Lord Jesus went about the Father's business during His earthly ministry (Luke 2:49). God wants us to be soul winners.

> Then Jesus came to them and said, "All authority in heaven and on earth has been given to me. Therefore go and make disciples of all nations, baptizing them in the name of the Father and of the Son and of the Holy Spirit, and teaching them to obey everything I have commanded you. And surely I am with you always, to the very end of the age." (Matthew 28:18–20)

The following phrase, "all authority in heaven and on earth has been given to me. Therefore go and make disciples of all nations," is worth highlighting from this scripture. It reveals that the mandate "to go make disciples of all nations" is on account of "all authority in heaven and on earth" that has been given to the Lord Jesus. This should inspire us to step out boldly in faith, knowing that our mandate has the full backing of the One who has all authority in heaven and on earth. We are not on our own. The Lord has assured us that He is with us always to the very end of the age. This is not a promise but a statement of fact. It is greatly comforting to know that the Lord Jesus is always with us. He will never leave us nor forsake us (Hebrews 13:5).

> The Lord himself goes before you and will be with you; he will never leave you nor forsake you. Do not be afraid; do not be discouraged. (Deuteronomy 31:8)

7. *The celebration feast*: "Let's have a feast and celebrate" (vs 23). The feast symbolizes the marriage supper of the Lamb, which

will take place soon in heaven. This is what the Bible says about the marriage supper of the Lamb:

> Let us rejoice and shout for joy [exulting and triumphant]! Let us celebrate and ascribe to Him glory and honor, for the marriage of the Lamb [at last] has come, and His bride has prepared herself. She has been permitted to dress in fine (radiant) linen, dazzling and white—for the fine linen is (signifies, represents) the righteousness (the upright, just, and godly living, deeds, and conduct, and right standing with God) of the saints (God's holy people). Then [the angel] said to me, Write this down: Blessed (happy, to be envied) are those who are summoned (invited, called) to the marriage supper of the Lamb. And he said to me [further], These are the true words (the genuine and exact declarations) of God. (Revelation 19:7–9 AMPC—Amplified Bible, Classic Edition)

This is when our union with Christ will be celebrated and consummated in heaven before the Father. This will be a lavish feast in heaven. The first of its kind in both heaven and earth. More insight into the nature of this feast is given in yet another parable of our Lord Jesus, which is discussed in depth in the next chapter. It will be an extravagant feast, hosted by the Almighty God Himself. During this period, the inhabitants of the earth will be going through the toughest time in the history of mankind, known as the great tribulation (Revelation 13:1–19 and Matthew 24:21–22). Following the marriage supper of the Lamb in heaven, the Lord Jesus and His saints will return to the earth to reign for a thousand years (millennial reign of Christ). The Lord will be physically seated in the temple in Jerusalem. Although the kingdom of God is a spiritual kingdom, but at that time, the kingdom will be both spiritual and physical. The Lord Jesus is coming back soon. We must be prepared to meet our Lord and King any time soon. This feast is discussed further in subsequent chapters of this book, including the relationship between the feast and a spectacular event that must happen here on earth, in the first instance, as the vehicle for transporting the invited guests to this celebration feast in heaven. This has been discussed in detail in the concluding chapter of this book.

8. *Note the order of items 2 to 7*. It is very interesting to see the perfect sequential order of all items given to the prodigal son from items 2 to 7 already discussed. There is no single item that is out of order, everything appears in the correct and perfect order, a divinely set order. This is never a coincidence but the miracle of God. Indeed, our God is perfect in all His ways! He is a God of order, justice, and equity.

- In *item 2*, the prodigal son returned home to his father, signifying repentance, which is the very first and foremost step to salvation. Without repentance, there is no remission of sins. Repentance always precedes the remission of sins.

> Peter replied, "Repent and be baptized, every one of you, in the name of Jesus Christ for the forgiveness of your sins. And you will receive the gift of the Holy Spirit." (Acts 2:38)

This is further shown in Luke 24:46–47 (NKJV), paying attention to the italicized words:

> Then He said to them, "Thus it is written, and thus it was necessary for the Christ to suffer and to rise from the dead the third day, and that *repentance* and *remission of sins* should be preached in His name to all nations, beginning at Jerusalem."

So repentance always comes first before anything else, and that is the case with the prodigal son.

- In *item 3*, the father hugged and kissed the prodigal son, signifying forgiveness and remission of his sins. Without repentance, there can never be the forgiveness of sins. So the prodigal son had to perform item 2 before qualifying for item 3, forgiveness and remission of sins.
- In *item 4*, the prodigal son was given the best robe, signifying righteousness and the gift of a new life in Christ. Until a man's sins are wiped away, he won't be justified before God. Justification qualifies a man to receive the righteousness of God as a gift, and that is the situation with the prodigal son in this parable. The father hugged and kissed him first before giving him the best robe. This could never have been done the other way around.
- In *item 5*, a ring was put on the finger of the prodigal son, signifying the power, authority, and dominion, which the believer has received in Christ, derived from the power of the Holy Spirit and the authority in the name of Jesus. Without receiving the righteousness of Christ in item 4, it is not possible to receive access to the power and authority in Christ. Item 4 must certainly come before item 5, and that is the same correct order in the parable.
- *Item 6* is the putting of shoes on the feet of the prodigal son, signifying the believer's mandate to witness for Christ and proclaim the gospel to the whole world, also known as the Great Commission. Without the empowerment of the Holy Spirit in item 5, it is not possible to effectively perform the Great Commission in item 6. The empowerment must precede the mandate for the Great Commission, and that is the situation with the prodigal son in this parable. The son received the ring before the shoes were put on his feet. The Holy Spirit empowerment of the believer must precede the mandate to witness for Christ by preaching the good news of peace to all men. Trying to go preach the

gospel before being empowered by the Holy Ghost is the same as the father asking the son to wear his shoes before giving him his ring. That's like putting the cart before the horse. That is not the way God planned it. Our God is a God of order.

- Finally, *item 7* is the feast to celebrate the safe return of the prodigal son home, signifying the marriage supper of the Lamb that will hold in heaven to celebrate the return of mankind back to God, following man's separation from God when Adam fell from grace. This feast will mark the celebration and consummation of the union between Christ and His church in the presence of His Father in heaven.

As I write this, I'm greatly overwhelmed with the profoundness of Christ's wisdom that has been displayed in telling this parable, which carries all the necessary details and components of God's salvation for mankind. The order is very pristine. *Items 3 to 5* combined is referred to as *salvation*, as can be seen in the Salvation Flow Chart in figure 1.

9. *The lost son reconnects to his father's wealth*: "My son," the father said, "you are always with me, and everything I have is yours" (vs 31). The quoted scripture in verse 31 relates to the first son, who, according to the father's response, owns the whole wealth that belongs to the father. This is very powerful. As has already been discussed, the first son symbolizes Israel, who are the children of Abraham. The blessing of God has been given to Abraham and his descendants by covenant. Therefore, the first son, Israel, has the blessing of God through Abraham. The prodigal son, symbolizing the Gentiles, has already squandered his own portion of inheritance in idolatry and paganism. Now he is back home, and because of the hug, kiss, best robe, and ring that were given to him by his father, he is now restored back to his father's estate as heir. This is mind-blowing! The lost son, through Christ, is back as an heir with full access to the

Father's estate. This is why Galatians 3:29 says, "If you belong to Christ, then you are Abraham's seed, and heirs according to the promise." Galatians 3:14 further says, "He redeemed us in order that the blessing given to Abraham might come to the Gentiles through Christ Jesus, so that by faith we might receive the promise of the Spirit." The lost son, because of Christ, is now reconnected to his Father's estate; he's now become an heir of his Father. This is like having your cake and eating it. The lost son originally ate his cake when he squandered his inheritance, but because of salvation through Christ, he is restored to the father's estate as an heir. This is why Romans 8:17 says, "Now if we are children, then we are heirs—heirs of God and coheirs with Christ, if indeed we share in his sufferings in order that we may also share in his glory." Through Christ, the Gentiles have become the children of God. They are reconnected to the blessing God gave to Abraham. The blessing of Abraham now belongs to both Jews and Gentiles through Christ. If both Jews and Gentiles are combined, then we have the whole of mankind. Therefore, all of mankind now have access to the blessing of Abraham through Christ. Now it can be seen the reason God told Abrahm that through his seed shall all the nations of the earth be blessed:

> In your seed all the nations of the earth shall be blessed, because you have obeyed My voice. (Genesis 22:18 NKJV)

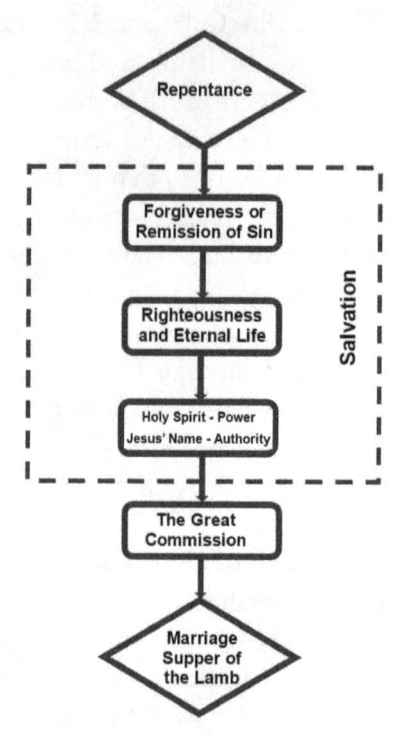

Figure 1: The Salvation Flow Chart

## The best robe, a great gift and a great mystery

> But the father said to his servants, "Quick! Bring the best robe and put it on him..." (Luke 15:22)

The best robe is a special robe given to the prodigal son. As earlier described, this symbolizes God's righteousness and eternal life, which are gifts given to the believer. The TPT rendering of Luke 15:22 gives further insight into the nature of this best robe; it's the same robe as the one being worn by the father, as can be seen in the italicized portion: "Turning to his servants, the father said, 'Quick, bring me the best robe, *my very own robe*, and I will place it on his shoulders...'" (Luke 15:22 TPT). This additional information about the robe is deeply illuminating. It shows that the best robe given to the prodigal son is the same as that of the father. That means, the righteousness and life received by the believer is the same as the righteousness and life of God. This is mind-blowing!

> But now apart from the law the righteousness of God has been made known, to which the Law and the Prophets testify. This righteousness is given through faith in Jesus Christ to all who believe. There is no difference between Jew and Gentile. (Romans 3:21–22)

## The best robe, a gift of righteousness

The best robe symbolizes the righteousness of God, which is only available in Christ Jesus. This righteousness is a gift from God for everyone that's in Christ, as clearly expressed in Romans 5:17, which says, "For if, by the trespass of the one man, death reigned through that one man, how much more will those who receive God's abundant provision of grace and of the gift of righteousness reign in life through the one man, Jesus Christ!" This righteousness is what the prodigal son received as the best robe. Everyone that comes to Christ receives this gift of righteousness. This is what gives the believer the right to stand blameless before God. It is not earned or worked for; it's a gift from God. The ascribing of God's righteousness to the believer is what gives him the right to stand uncondemned before God. The righteousness of God gives the believer access to the full package of salvation and life in Christ Jesus. This is the reason why the prodigal son was first given the best robe before receiving all other items: the ring, shoes, and celebration feast. Righteousness is the foundation of the Christian life; without it, no man can ever receive anything else in Christ. No wonder the psalmist declared, "Righteousness and justice are the foundation of your throne; love and faithfulness go before you" (Psalm 89:14). As seen in the parable, the best robe (symbolizing God's righteousness and eternal life) comes before the ring on his finger (symbolizing power, authority, and dominion). It comes before the shoes on his feet (symbolizing the Great Commission). It comes before the celebration feast (symbolizing the marriage supper of the Lamb). A man can't receive any of these until he's first made right with God through the gift of righteousness that's freely given to everyone that believes in Jesus Christ. Righteousness gives man the right standing before God. The righteousness of God in Christ Jesus is possible because of justification, which means to be declared not guilty. This is as a result of the substitutionary work of Christ on the cross, where Christ took our place of sin and condemnation, declaring us not guilty. This opens the way for man to have access to the righteousness of God. Justification comes only by faith in the finished work of Christ. This is why Romans 5:1–2 says, "Therefore, since we have been justified through faith, we have peace with God through our Lord Jesus Christ, through whom we have gained access by faith into this grace in which we now stand." Justification opened the door wide for mankind to fully access the righteousness of God, which is in Christ Jesus. All that's needed is for everyman to repent and receive the remission of sins. This was the case with the prodigal son. By virtue of his genuine repentance, by returning home to his father, he received the complete remission of sin when his father hugged and kissed him. This was reconciliation and peace with his father. This is why our earlier scripture in Romans 5:1 says, "Therefore, since we have been justified through faith, we have peace with God through our Lord Jesus Christ." This therefore opened the door for the prodigal son to receive the best robe (righteousness and eternal life), the ring (power, authority, and dominion), shoes (the right to witness for Christ), and the future celebration feast (the marriage supper of the Lamb in heaven). Faith in the finished work of Christ is what brings justification and the resultant righteousness to the life of anyone that believes. This aligns with 2 Corinthians 5:21, which says, "God made him who had no sin to be sin for us, so that in him we might become the righteousness of God." Although righteousness is a gift, freely available to mankind, for any man to qualify for this gift, he must repent and turn to God by receiving His Son, Jesus Christ, as clearly expressed in Acts 3:19–20, saying, "Repent, then, and turn to God, so that your sins may be wiped out, that times of refreshing may come from the Lord, and that he may send the Messiah, who has been appointed for you—even Jesus." The Lord Jesus Christ is the Messiah. It is only through Him and by believing in His name that salvation is available to mankind. The righteousness of God is only found in Jesus Christ. He is the way, the truth, and the life, and no one can come to the Father except by Him alone (John 14:6). While righteousness comes freely as a gift, the Bible encourages us to live accordingly. The believer must live a life that's consistent with the righteousness of God in Christ Jesus. This is the proof that we are truly righteous when we live and practice righteousness. This is why 1 John 3:7–8 (NKJV) says, "Little children, let no one deceive you. He who practices righteousness is righteous, just as He is righteous. He who sins is of the devil, for the devil has sinned from the beginning. For this purpose the Son of God was manifested, that He might destroy the works of the devil." Having received the righteousness of God in Christ Jesus, sin should no longer reign in the believer's life, as Christ has been manifested in him, destroying the sinful works of the devil. The believer must now walk by faith and practice the good works of righteousness. The life of righteousness is only lived by faith in the finished work of Christ and by the power of the Holy Spirit.

## The best robe, a gift of eternal life

The best robe also symbolizes eternal life, which is the very life and essence of God. John 3:16 says, "For God so loved the world that he gave his one and only Son, that whoever believes in him shall not perish but have eternal life." So just like righteousness, eternal life is also a gift given to anyone who is in Christ Jesus. This is why Romans 6:23 says, "For the wages of sin is death, but the gift of God is eternal life in Christ Jesus our Lord." Eternal life is the divine life of God, which is translated from the Greek word *zoe*. This is the very life and essence of God, which is given as a gift to anyone that receives Jesus Christ as Lord and Savior. This divine life is from God, given by His one and only Son, Jesus Christ. It's the best and greatest type of life there is in heaven and on earth. This is why 1 John 5:11–12 says, "And this is the testimony: God has given us eternal life, and this life is in his Son. Whoever has the Son has life; whoever does not have the Son of God does not have life." It is God Himself who has given us this life, and it's made available in Jesus Christ, the Son of God. Anyone that has Christ has this life; anyone that does not have Christ does not have this life. This is the significance of the best robe. The prodigal son, the repented Gentile, has received Christ and now has eternal life. The one in Christ has received the same life as God, eternal life, which is His very own robe. This is why the apostle Peter, writing in 2 Peter 1:3 (NKJV), declared that "through these you may be partakers of the divine nature, having escaped the corruption that is in the world through lust." Having the same life as God, eternal life, makes the believer a partaker of the divine nature. This is so beautiful! That word *partaker* used in the passage is translated from the Greek word *koinonos*, which means a partner, an associate, a companion, a carrier, a sharer, a comrade, etc.

The one who is in Christ has received eternal life and has now become a partaker, associate, carrier, and sharer of God's divine nature. This is what the prodigal son received by virtue of the best robe that was given to him as gift. This gift is only available in Christ. Father God always wants His children to be aware that He's given them the best robe, which is his very own robe. He wants them to be conscious that they have the same life and righteousness as Him. The apostle John wrote by the Spirit to all believers in Christ Jesus, saying, "I write these things to you who believe in the name of the Son of God so that you may know that you have eternal life" (1 John 5:13). The word *know* in that passage is translated from the Greek word *eido*, which means to be aware, be conscious, take notice of something, turn your eye and mind to see something, observe and pay attention to something, etc.

Father God wants us to know that we have eternal life. He wants us to be aware and conscious that we have the same life as Him. The Bible encourages believers to turn their eyes and minds and pay attention to the fact that they have eternal life in Christ Jesus. This is akin to the father reminding the prodigal son that he's been given the best robe, the father's very own robe. He wants him to be aware and conscious of this fact. The reason is because without the prodigal son being conscious that he has the best robe, which is the same as the father's, he's likely to take it for granted and be reckless with the robe. The father wants the prodigal son to take responsibility for maintaining the best robe that has been given to him as gift. The father wants him to keep the best robe clean and always protected, away from the stains of sin and filthiness. In the same vein, the believer has received eternal life, God's own very life. The Lord wants us to be aware and conscious of this divine life that we carry so that we can live accordingly. To whom much is given, much is expected. Because of this great divine life in us, God expects us to live a life that's consistent thereof, a life that's sanctified, pure, and holy, a life that's pleasing unto God, as encouraged in the living word of God, where it says, "Therefore, I urge you, brothers and sisters, in view of God's mercy, to offer your bodies as a living sacrifice, holy and pleasing to God—this is your true and proper worship" (Romans 12:1), a life that's fully and absolutely yielded to Him, His word, and divine will, a life that is completely surrendered and submitted to the authority of His word and Holy Spirit. This is why He wants us to be conscious that we have eternal life.

## The best robe, a great mystery

The best robe, which symbolizes both righteousness and eternal life, is a great mystery. This mystery is known as the mystery of Christ. From the word of God, we know that Christ is our righteousness. Christ has become our righteousness (1 Corinthians 1:30). He is *"the Lord our righteousness"* (Jeremiah 33:16 NKJV). Similarly, Christ is our life (Colossians 3:4). Jesus Christ is the way, the truth, and the life (John 14:6). From John 1:4, we know "in him was life, and that life was the light of all mankind." This eternal life, that was from the beginning, was manifested to mankind as Jesus Christ, as clearly expressed in the scripture that says, "The life appeared; we have seen it and testify to it, and we proclaim to you the eternal life, which was with the Father and has appeared to us" (1 John 1:2 NLT). Since the best robe is righteousness and eternal life and Christ is our righteousness and eternal life, therefore the best robe is Christ. What a great mystery! We can now see that when the prodigal son repented and returned to his father, the very first gift the father gave to him was the best robe, which represents Christ. When a sinner returns to God, he receives Christ. This is the way of salvation. That individual becomes a new man, having the life and righteousness of God. This is why the word of God says, "If a man belongs to Christ, he is a new person. The old life is gone. New life has begun" (2 Corinthians 5:17 NLV—New Life Version). Christ is the believer's best robe. This is why Romans 13:14 says, "Rather, clothe yourselves with the Lord Jesus Christ, and do not think about how to gratify the desires of the flesh." The believer has put on Christ, like a garment, which is the best robe. He's clothed himself with Christ, as powerfully expressed in Galatians 3:27, which says, "For all of you who were baptized into Christ have clothed yourselves with Christ." The prodigal son received the best robe first before receiving the ring. In the same vein, everyone must first receive Christ before they can receive the power and authority that's in Christ. We see this happen in the Acts of the Apostles, when the seven sons of Sceva tried to manifest the authority in the name of Christ (the ring) when they have not received Christ (the best robe).

> Some Jews who went around driving out evil spirits tried to invoke the name of the Lord Jesus over those who were demon-possessed. They would say, "In the name of the Jesus whom Paul preaches, I command you to come out." Seven sons of Sceva, a Jewish chief priest, were doing this. One day the evil spirit answered them, "Jesus I know, and Paul I know about, but who are you?" Then the man who had the evil spirit jumped on them and overpowered them all. He gave them such a beating that they ran out of the house naked and bleeding. (Acts 19:13–16)

The sons of Sceva couldn't cast out demons in the name of the Lord Jesus; instead they were beaten mercilessly because it is not possible for the one who is not saved to exercise the authority that's in

Christ. That is like having the ring without first having the best robe. You can't have the ring before the best robe. It is not possible to have the authority that's available in Christ without first giving your life to Christ. However, it's possible to receive the best robe and yet not have the ring. This is the sad and unfortunate situation with many believers today. Many are genuinely in Christ (having the best robe) but without the infilling of the Holy Spirit (the ring) who's the One that gives power to the believer, according to Acts 1:8, which says, "But you will receive power when the Holy Spirit comes on you..." We also see this happen in the Acts of the Apostles, when the apostle Paul found some believers in Ephesus who never heard about the Holy Ghost, let alone receive Him.

> While Apollos was at Corinth, Paul took the road through the interior and arrived at Ephesus. There he found some disciples and asked them, "Did you receive the Holy Spirit when you believed?" They answered, "No, we have not even heard that there is a Holy Spirit." So Paul asked, "Then what baptism did you receive?" "John's baptism," they replied. Paul said, "John's baptism was a baptism of repentance. He told the people to believe in the one coming after him, that is, in Jesus." On hearing this, they were baptized in the name of the Lord Jesus. When Paul placed his hands on them, the Holy Spirit came on them, and they spoke in tongues and prophesied. There were about twelve men in all. (Acts 19:1–7)

Unfortunately, this is the sad situation with so many believers around the world today. Many have genuinely received Christ and yet cannot exercise the authority in the name of Jesus. The reason for this spiritual anomaly is ignorance of the word of God. The apostle Paul noticed this ignorance in the lives of these twelve believers that were in Ephesus. He quickly remedied the situation by educating them with God's word, as well as praying for them through the laying of hands to impart them with the Holy Ghost. The apostle Paul knew it was a huge risk to let those twelve believers return home the same way he met them. In the end, the twelve believers gladly received the Holy Ghost, speaking in tongues and prophesying. What a joy to behold! Today, many believers cannot exercise the power of the Holy Ghost and the authority in the name of Jesus because of this same ignorance, not knowing the Scriptures. This is why the Lord Almighty, speaking through the prophet Hosea, said, "My people are destroyed from lack of knowledge" (Hosea 4:6). Our Lord Jesus, also, once replied to the Sadducees, saying, "You are in error because you do not know the Scriptures or the power of God" (Matthew 22:29). The remedy for this spiritual anomaly is to genuinely hunger for God's word and thirst for His Holy Spirit. Thirst passionately for His power and glory, like the psalmist when he said, "O God, You are my God; early will I seek You; my soul thirsts for You; my flesh longs for You in a dry and thirsty land where there is no water. So I have looked for You in the sanctuary, to see Your power and Your glory" (Psalm 63:1–2 NKJV). The psalmist further reiterated this by saying, "As the deer pants for the water brooks, so pants my soul for You, O God. My soul thirsts for God, for the living God. When shall I come and appear before God?" (Psalm 42:1–2 NKJV). It is indeed a noble thing to hunger and thirst for God. The Lord has assured us in His holy word that we would find Him when we seek Him wholeheartedly.

> You will seek me and find me when you seek me with all your heart. (Jeremiah 29:13)

Similarly, the Lord Jesus gave an open invitation to anyone that dares to thirst, saying, "'Let anyone who is thirsty come to me and drink. Whoever believes in me, as Scripture has said, rivers of living water will flow from within them.' By this he meant the Spirit, whom those who believed in him were later to receive. Up to that time the Spirit had not been given since Jesus had not yet been glorified" (John 7:37–39). Now that the Lord Jesus has been glorified, the Holy Spirit is freely available to everyone that believes. All that is needed is a hunger and a thirst. It is a blessing to hunger and thirst for God, for righteousness. The Lord has assured us that those who hunger and thirst would be filled. Blessed are they that hunger and thirst for righteousness, for they will be filled (Matthew 5:6).

## The best robe and the ring, a game changer for mankind

As we begin to bring this chapter to a close, having fully discussed the various items that were given to the prodigal son, it is worth highlighting that the combination of the best robe and the ring is an eternal game changer for mankind. This combination of the best robe and the ring results in Christ's righteousness, eternal life, power, and authority. This combination is a game changer for all humankind, giving the ultimate dominion to man. This is God's will for mankind and the reason for giving us His One and only Son. The Lord Jesus came to save and restore all of mankind to God. He didn't come for a particular nation or group of people but for the whole world of men. God gave His beloved Son to the world, who died to save all mankind.

## Summary

The Parable of the Prodigal Son has been unveiled in this chapter. The underlying story indicates the return of the Gentiles to God through Christ. The Gentiles, who were alienated from the commonwealth of God, are now reconciled to God through Christ Jesus. Before now, the covenant of God's blessing, given to the patriarch Abraham, was only available to the Jews. However, through Christ, the Gentiles have been reconnected to the blessing of Abraham. Like the Jews, the Gentiles, through Christ, have now become the seed of Abraham. When a Gentile repents and turns to God, he's given the gifts of righteousness and eternal life. The power of the Holy Spirit, as well as the authority to use the name of Jesus, are given to him. With these, he's equipped and empowered to witness for Christ in the Great Commission. Finally, the repented Gentile awaits the marriage supper of the Lamb in heaven. This feast is the official consummation and celebration of the return of mankind back to God. The best robe, given by the father to the prodigal son, was further discussed. The best robe is seen to symbolize the gifts of righteousness and eternal life, both of which are freely received when any man receives Christ as his Lord and Savior. This chapter looked deep into how the best robe is a great gift from God. Since Christ is both our righteousness and eternal life, this chapter further unveiled the best robe as a great mystery, known as the mystery of Christ. The best robe is therefore seen to be a great gift and a great mystery, symbolizing Christ. Finally, it is deeply illuminating to see the combination of the best robe and the ring, symbolizing Christ and the ultimate dominion that has been given in Christ. This is a game changer for all mankind. The Parable of the Prodigal Son and its hidden message have been summarized using the flow chart in figure 2 below. The Lord Jesus gave us more information about the best robe and its future implications to mankind in yet another parable of the Lord. This is discussed in depth in the next chapter.

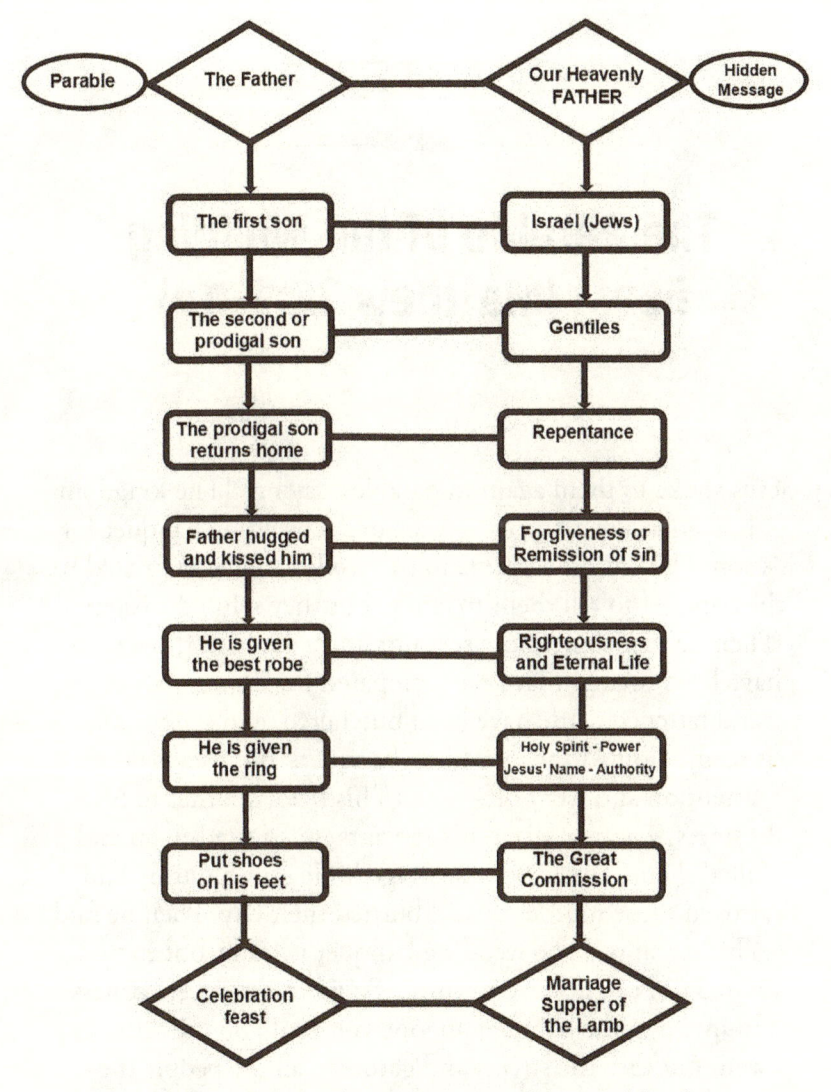

```
  Parable        The Father            Our Heavenly         Hidden
                                          FATHER            Message

              The first son    ———    Israel (Jews)

              The second or    ———    Gentiles
              prodigal son

              The prodigal son ———    Repentance
              returns home

              Father hugged    ———    Forgiveness or
              and kissed him          Remission of sin

              He is given      ———    Righteousness
              the best robe           and Eternal Life

              He is given      ———    Holy Spirit - Power
              the ring                Jesus' Name - Authority

              Put shoes        ———    The Great
              on his feet             Commission

              Celebration             Marriage
              feast                   Supper of
                                      the Lamb
```

Figure 2: Flow Chart Summary of the Parable of the Prodigal Son and Its Hidden Message

# CHAPTER 3

# The Parable of the Wedding Feast (Matthew 22:1–14)

Jesus spoke to them again in parables, saying: "The kingdom of heaven is like a king who prepared a wedding banquet for his son. He sent his servants to those who had been invited to the banquet to tell them to come, but they refused to come. Then he sent some more servants and said, 'Tell those who have been invited that I have prepared my dinner: My oxen and fattened cattle have been butchered, and everything is ready. Come to the wedding banquet.' But they paid no attention and went off—one to his field, another to his business. The rest seized his servants, mistreated them and killed them. The king was enraged. He sent his army and destroyed those murderers and burned their city. Then he said to his servants, 'The wedding banquet is ready, but those I invited did not deserve to come. So go to the street corners and invite to the banquet anyone you find.' So the servants went out into the streets and gathered all the people they could find, the bad as well as the good, and the wedding hall was filled with guests. But when the king came in to see the guests, he noticed a man there who was not wearing wedding clothes. He asked, 'How did you get in here without wedding clothes, friend?' The man was speechless. Then the king told the attendants, 'Tie him hand and foot, and throw him outside, into the darkness, where there will be weeping and gnashing of teeth.' For many are invited, but few are chosen."

—Matthew 22:1–14

This is yet another powerful parable of our Lord Jesus Christ. This parable gives further insight into two important areas of the Parable of the Prodigal Son earlier discussed in chapter 2. First, we are given in-depth knowledge and insight into the nature of the celebration feast that the father organized to welcome the prodigal son home. This feast is the same as the wedding feast in this parable. The fattened cattle that was slaughtered to prepare the wedding meal is the same as the one which was slaughtered in chapter 2 to welcome the prodigal son home, when the father said to his servants, "'Bring the fattened calf and kill it. Let's have a feast and celebrate. For this son of mine was dead and is alive again; he was lost and is found.' So they began to celebrate" (Luke 15:23–24).

The celebration and wedding feasts both symbolize the same thing, the marriage supper of the Lamb, which is recorded in the book of Revelation, where it says, "'Let us rejoice and be glad and give him glory! For the wedding of the Lamb has come, and his bride has made herself ready. Fine linen, bright and clean, was given her to wear.' (Fine linen stands for the righteous acts of God's holy people.) Then the angel said to me, 'Write this: Blessed are those who are invited to the wedding supper of the Lamb!' And he added, 'These are the true words of God'" (Revelation 19:7–9).

This is a huge wedding feast that God the Father has arranged for Christ and His bride in heaven. I love the TPT rendering of Matthew 22:2, saying, "There once was a king who arranged an *extravagant wedding feast* for his son." Indeed, the marriage supper of the Lamb is an extravagant wedding feast. It will be the feast of all feasts. In short, this will be the greatest and most extravagant wedding feast that's ever been witnessed in heaven and on earth. It will be lavish, extravagant party, organized by the Almighty God Himself. Our God is the King of kings and Lord of lords. He is the ultimate royalty and monarch of the universe. If mere human royals know how to arrange extravagant wedding feasts for their kids, one can only imagine what a feast that's been organized by the monarch of the universe Himself for His kids would look like. It's the type of feast that no human or angel has ever witnessed anywhere in the universe. Such lavish feast never existed; it is without precedence. It will be the ultimate, quintessential royal wedding feast. You mustn't miss this wedding feast!

## Unveiling the Parable of the Wedding Feast

Let us begin by first unveiling the characters in this parable:

1. *The king that prepared the wedding feast for his son* symbolizes the King of kings, the Lord God Almighty. Our God is the King of all the earth. He rules forever and ever.

   > For God is the King of all the earth; sing to him a psalm of praise. (Psalm 47:7)

   Our God is the King of glory, according to the psalmist, when he asked, "Who is he, this King of glory? The Lord Almighty—he is the King of glory" (Psalm 24:10).

   > Now to the King eternal, immortal, invisible, the only God, be honor and glory for ever and ever. Amen. (1 Timothy 1:17)

2. *The son, for whom the wedding feast is prepared*, symbolizes the one and only begotten Son of God, our Lord Jesus Christ. Our Lord Jesus Christ is the bridegroom of the church, which is His bride. John the Baptist gave this testimony about the Lord Jesus as the bridegroom, saying, "The bride belongs to the bridegroom. The friend who attends the bridegroom waits and listens for him, and is full of joy when he hears the bridegroom's voice. That joy is mine, and it is now complete" (John 3:29). What a beautiful testimony by John the Baptist! By this, John was referring to the

Lord Jesus as the bridegroom and himself as the friend of the bridegroom. Similarly, when some people came to ask the Lord Jesus why His disciples were not fasting the way John's disciples and the Pharisees did regularly, "Jesus answered, 'How can the guests of the bridegroom fast while he is with them? They cannot, so long as they have him with them. But the time will come when the bridegroom will be taken from them, and on that day they will fast'" (Mark 2:19–20). By this, the Lord Jesus was referring to Himself as the bridegroom. In Ephesians 5:25–32, the apostle Paul, by the spirit of God, unveiled the great mystery behind the relationship between Christ and His church, where Christ is the husband (bridegroom) and the church His wife (bride). The apostle John gave us very clear accounts about the bridegroom and His bride in the book of Revelation. The first is found in Revelation 19, where it says, "Let us rejoice and be glad and give him glory! For the wedding of the Lamb has come, and his bride has made herself ready" (Revelation 19:7). This very wedding event in Revelation 19:7 is the same as the wedding feast in this parable. Both are one and the same. The second account is given in Revelation 21, where it says, "I saw the Holy City, the new Jerusalem, coming down out of heaven from God, prepared as a bride beautifully dressed for her husband. One of the seven angels who had the seven bowls full of the seven last plagues came and said to me, 'Come, I will show you the bride, the wife of the Lamb.' And he carried me away in the Spirit to a mountain great and high, and showed me the Holy City, Jerusalem, coming down out of heaven from God" (Revelation 21:2, 9–10).

3. *The servants sent to invite the guests. They seized some of his servants, mistreated them, and killed them.* The servants symbolize God's prophets that were sent across different eras and generations. Some were mistreated, and others were killed. For example, John the Baptist, one of such prophets, was beheaded by Herod. The Lord Jesus alluded to these murderous acts that were committed against the prophets of God across different generations and eras. One day, while replying to the experts in the

law, the Lord Jesus said, "Woe to you, because you build tombs for the prophets, and it was your ancestors who killed them. So you testify that you approve of what your ancestors did; they killed the prophets, and you build their tombs. Because of this, God in his wisdom said, 'I will send them prophets and apostles, some of whom they will kill and others they will persecute.' Therefore this generation will be held responsible for the blood of all the prophets that has been shed since the beginning of the world, from the blood of Abel to the blood of Zechariah, who was killed between the altar and the sanctuary. Yes, I tell you, this generation will be held responsible for it all" (Luke 11:47–51). On another occasion, the Lord Jesus repeated the same to the Pharisees and teachers of the law, saying, "Woe to you, teachers of the law and Pharisees, you hypocrites! You build tombs for the prophets and decorate the graves of the righteous. And you say, 'If we had lived in the days of our ancestors, we would not have taken part with them in shedding the blood of the prophets.' So you testify against yourselves that you are the descendants of those who murdered the prophets. Go ahead, then, and complete what your ancestors started!" (Matthew 23:29–32). The Lord restated this in some of His most touching words to the Jews when they rejected Him in Jerusalem, saying, "Jerusalem, Jerusalem, you who kill the prophets and stone those sent to you, how often I have longed to gather your children together, as a hen gathers her chicks under her wings, and you were not willing. Look, your house is left to you desolate" (Matthew 23:37–38). Before his martyrdom, Stephen said the same to the people, saying, "You stiff-necked people! Your hearts and ears are still uncircumcised. You are just like your ancestors: You always resist the Holy Spirit! Was there ever a prophet your ancestors did not persecute? They even killed those who predicted the coming of the righteous One. And now you have betrayed and murdered him" (Acts 7:51–52).

4. *The original guests that were invited to the wedding* symbolize Israel or the Jews. This is the first son in the Parable of the Prodigal Son earlier discussed. The Jews were the original peo-

ple to be invited to this wedding; however, as a nation, they rejected God's one and only Son, Jesus Christ. Consequently, the kingdom was taken away from them and given to a people, the church, majorly made up of Gentiles, who will produce the fruit of righteousness of the kingdom, according to the words of our Lord Jesus Christ, when He said, "Therefore I tell you that the kingdom of God will be taken away from you and given to a people who will produce its fruit" (Matthew 21:43).

5. *The good and bad people invited* symbolize the whole world, comprising both the Jews and Gentiles, all of mankind comprising of both good and bad people. This is how the invitation was extended to the Gentiles, resulting in the offer of salvation to all mankind, made up of both Jews and Gentiles. Before His glorious ascension, the Lord Jesus commanded His disciples, saying, "Go into all the world and preach the gospel to all creation. Whoever believes and is baptized will be saved, but whoever does not believe will be condemned" (Mark 16:15–16). This invitation is to all mankind, comprising of both the good, the bad, and the ugly. No one, no matter how bad or ugly, is exempted from the invitation of salvation in Christ Jesus. The gospel of Christ is to all men and all creation. The invitation is to all people, both good and bad, Jew and Gentile. Writing by the spirit of God, the apostle Paul said, "For the grace of God has appeared that offers salvation to all people" (Titus 2:11). The good and bad invited to the wedding is the whole world. No one is left out.

6. *The murderers, whose city was burned down,* symbolize the Jews (killers of God's prophets), whose city, Jerusalem, was destroyed and burned down by the Babylonians, including the destruction of the city and temple in AD 70 by Roman military. One of such several examples in scripture says, "On the tenth day of the fifth month, in the nineteenth year of Nebuchadnezzar king of Babylon, Nebuzaradan commander of the imperial guard, who served the king of Babylon, came to Jerusalem. He set fire to the temple of the Lord, the royal palace and all the houses of Jerusalem. Every important building he burned down" (Jeremiah 52:12–13).

7. *The attendants that tied the speechless man's hand and foot and threw him outside into outer darkness* symbolize the angels of the Lord. These angels were seen performing similar task, throwing the wicked into blazing furnace in the Parable of the Net in chapter 1, where it says, "This is how it will be at the end of the age. The angels will come and separate the wicked from the righteous and throw them into the blazing furnace, where there will be weeping and gnashing of teeth" (Matthew 13:49–50). Similarly, the same is seen in the Parable of the Wheat in the Field, which says, "As the weeds are pulled up and burned in the fire, so it will be at the end of the age. The Son of Man will send out his angels, and they will weed out of his kingdom everything that causes sin and all who do evil. They will throw them into the blazing furnace, where there will be weeping and gnashing of teeth" (Matthew 13:41–42).
8. *The speechless man that wasn't wearing a wedding garment* symbolizes an individual that stands in his own righteousness. This is very crucial and is discussed further below.

## Important points to note from the Parable of the Wedding Feast

1. *The wedding feast.* This wedding feast is the same as the celebration feast in the Parable of the Prodigal Son. They both symbolize the marriage supper of the Lamb, which is recorded in Revelation 19:7–9. This will be an extravagant wedding feast in heaven. The fattened cattle that was seen in the Parable of the Prodigal Son in chapter 2 is also seen here in this Parable of the Wedding Feast. Both feasts are one and the same. What makes a feast is the food. This will be a big feast in heaven, and there will be lots of food and drinks, and the Almighty Father Himself will be present.
2. *The wedding garment.* The wedding garment in this parable is the same as the best robe in the Parable of the Prodigal Son. It symbolizes the righteousness of God and eternal life, representing Christ. At the wedding feast, the king came around

for fellowship to have comradeship and communion with the invited guests. They were all wearing the same wedding garment as him, which is the righteousness of God that's only found in Christ Jesus. Earlier in Revelation 19:7 (KJV), we read, "Let us be glad and rejoice, and give honor to him: for the marriage of the Lamb is come, and his wife hath made herself ready. And to her was *granted* that she should be arrayed in fine linen, clean and white: *for the fine linen is the righteousness of saints*." The first italicized word indicates that the wife or bride was granted that she should be arrayed in fine linen, signifying that the fine linen was freely granted to her as a gift. We get further insight from the italicized portion, which shows that this fine linen that was granted to the bride is the righteousness of saints. This corroborates everything that's been said about the wedding garment and best robe being the same thing, which is the righteousness of God in Christ Jesus, and is given to every believer as a gift. Fellowship is a friendly association, especially with people who share one's interests. The king came around for fellowship with the guests since they all share the same interest of righteousness (wedding garment) as him. This is why the Scriptures make us know that we have become partakers of God's divine nature, associates of the God kind (2 Peter 1:4). Christ, through His work of salvation for mankind, has brought man into fellowship with the Father. This is our highest calling as children of God (2 Corinthians 13:14). The apostle John wrote in 1 John 1:3, saying, "We proclaim to you what we have seen and heard, so that you also may have fellowship with us. And our fellowship is with the Father and with his Son, Jesus Christ."

3. *Every man can only stand before God in Christ's righteousness alone.* In the previous chapter, four types of righteousness were identified and discussed. Only the righteousness of God in Christ Jesus, symbolized by the best robe, is tenable before God. All other types of righteousness are untenable. The speechless man at the wedding banquet is wearing his own righteousness. He's not wearing the righteousness of God in Christ Jesus.

4. *When a man stands before God.* On that day, when men stand before their Maker, many will be speechless when they find themselves standing in their own righteousness, which is like a filthy rag before God (Isaiah 64:6).
5. *The speechless man found himself wearing rag before the Lord.* The rag represents sin, shame, sorrow, dishonor, and loss. Although the speechless man found himself amid God's children, but he wasn't wearing the righteousness of God, he wore his own self-righteousness, which was a filthy rag before God. That man was possibly a preacher, singer, or a well-known elder in his church, but he didn't have the righteousness of Christ. He wasn't truly repented of his sins. He wasn't living a life that's consistent with true righteous living. He was in church but not in touch with God. He wasn't obedient to the word of God. He was one of those churchgoers that the Lord Jesus referred to when He said, "Why do you call me, 'Lord, Lord,' and do not do what I say?" (Luke 6:46). He further described them, saying, "These people honor me with their lips, but their hearts are far from me. They worship me in vain; their teachings are merely human rules" (Matthew 15:8). The Lord Jesus wants His children to live in total obedience to His word. Total surrender and obedience to God's word is the epitome of sonship in the kingdom of God. It doesn't matter how many great miracles a believer may have performed in the name of Jesus, if that believer doesn't live in absolute obedience to God's word while fully yielded to His Holy Spirit, doing the will of the Father, the Lord Jesus says that person will not enter the kingdom of heaven.

> Not everyone who says to me, "Lord, Lord," will enter the kingdom of heaven, but only the one who does the will of my Father who is in heaven. Many will say to me on that day, "Lord, Lord, did we not prophesy in your name and in your name drive out demons and in your name perform many miracles?" Then I will tell them

plainly, "I never knew you. Away from me, you evildoers!" (Matthew 7:21–23)

6. *Many are called, but only few are chosen.* The invitation to attend this wedding feast is open to all mankind. The whole world is called and invited, but only those who respond by faith by receiving Jesus Christ as their Lord and Savior, living accordingly in total submission and obedience to His word and Holy Spirit, are the chosen ones.

> For the grace of God has appeared that offers salvation to all people. It teaches us to say 'No' to ungodliness and worldly passions, and to live self-controlled, upright and godly lives in this present age, while we wait for the blessed hope—the appearing of the glory of our great God and Savior, Jesus Christ, who gave Himself for us to redeem us from all wickedness and to purify for Himself a people that are his very own, eager to do what is good. (Titus 2:11–14)

Although everyone that believes in Christ is called a believer; nevertheless, only those that are yielded to His word and continually led by the Holy Spirit are the children of God, as clearly expressed in Romans 8:14, saying, "For those who are led by the spirit of God are the children of God." God wants us to be yielded to His word and Holy Spirit. He always wants His children to be led by His spirit. This is the hallmark of sonship in His kingdom. The whole world is called and invited to this wedding feast, but only those that respond by faith, by accepting this invitation and living accordingly, are the chosen ones. Everyone is given the opportunity to be invited to this wedding feast. It is up to that individual to accept or reject the invitation. This is the reason why we are called to be Christ's witnesses, to tell the untold about this good news of salvation in Christ Jesus our Lord. This is the Great Commission that has been given to us as shoes on our feet, as earlier discussed in the previous chapter. For those that have accepted this invitation, the believers, it is up to them individually to decide whether they want to abide by the instructions and attire that have been provided for this great wedding feast. The instruction is very clear: The only attire allowed is the best robe, which is the righteousness of God in Christ Jesus. Without Christ's righteousness, no man can be chosen for this wedding feast. The instruction manual for the wedding is the Bible, the holy word of God, which must be obeyed in totality. Partial obedience of God's word is not acceptable. In this kingdom, partial obedience is the same as disobedience. Finally, those that have accepted to attend this wedding feast must be led and abide by the instructions from the indwelling Holy Spirit all the time.

7. *The speechless man was bound hand and foot, taken away, and cast into outer darkness. There shall be weeping and gnashing of teeth.* The situation here is a potential reality for any believer. Everyone must stand firm in the faith by totally obeying God's word and being led by His Holy Spirit. The notion that "once saved, always saved" is a big lie from hell; it has no basis in the word of God. Every believer must "contend earnestly for the faith which was once for all delivered to the saints" (Jude 1:3 NKJV). Being a follower of Christ is a fight, the reason we are called soldiers of Christ. The word of God enjoins us to "fight the good fight of faith, and to lay hold on eternal life" (1 Timothy 6:12 NKJV). The phrase "lay hold on eternal life" implies that one can let eternal life slip away if one refuses to keep holding onto it. This is why Philippians 2:12 (NKJV) says, "Therefore, my beloved, as you have always obeyed, not as in my presence only, but now much more in my absence, *work out your own salvation with fear and trembling.*" The speechless man in this parable refused to work out his salvation with fear and trembling. He was casual with God and the things of God, not taking his spiritual life seriously. This is the same situation with many believers today. Many blatantly and flagrantly go against the instruction of God in the Bible, doing things that are pleasing to them and men. Many believers and church leaders seek the approval and

applaud of the world in their dealings with God. They are willing to seriously compromise on their faith and the word of God just to get the praise of men. No wonder John 12:43 says, "For they loved human praise more than praise from God." Their interest is to live for men and please men; they are men pleasers. They have forgotten that Christ is the only one that we are called to live for, as the word of God says, "He died for all, so that those who live should no longer live for themselves, but *only for him* who died and was raised to life for their sake" (2 Corinthians 5:15 GNT—Good News Translation). Christ is the only One we are required to live for. This should guide everything you do and the way you live your life daily. The speechless man in this parable did not live for Christ; he probably lived for himself or for others he sought their praise. Having lived as a false believer, he stood speechless when faced with his Maker and ended up being bound hand and foot, taken away, and cast into outer darkness, where there shall be weeping and gnashing of teeth. So for a believer to avoid this, being his experience on that day, that believer must remain fully rooted and grounded in Christ alone. If you think you are standing, you should be cautious not to fall.

> So anyone who thinks he is standing strong should be careful not to fall. (1 Corinthians 10:12 ICB—International Children's Bible)

Watch and pray always that you fall not into temptation, as instructed by the Master in Matthew 26:41. Absolute surrender and obedience to God, His word, and Holy Spirit are paramount ways of building our lives wisely on Christ, the solid rock. The Lord Jesus spoke clearly about this when He said, "Therefore everyone who hears these words of mine and puts them into practice is like a wise man who built his house on the rock. The rain came down, the streams rose, and the winds blew and beat against that house; yet it did not fall, because it had its foundation on the rock. But everyone who hears these words of mine and does not put them into practice is like a foolish man who built his house on sand. The rain came down, the streams rose, and the winds blew and beat against that house, and it fell with a great crash" (Matthew 7:24–27). Learn to obey and practice the word of God. This is one great way of abiding in Him. The Lord wants us to abide absolutely in Him. The one who abides in Him remains securely rooted in Him and will bear much fruit. This is why the Lord said, "I am the vine; you are the branches. If you remain in me and I in you, you will bear much fruit; apart from me you can do nothing. If you do not remain in me, you are like a branch that is thrown away and withers; such branches are picked up, thrown into the fire and burned. If you remain in me and my words remain in you, ask whatever you wish, and it will be done for you. This is to my Father's glory, that you bear much fruit, showing yourselves to be my disciples" (John 15:5–8).

## The wedding bride, a great mystery

In this parable, there is the wedding groom and the invited guests, but there is no mention of the wedding bride. Can there ever be a wedding feast without a bride? No! So why isn't there a bride in this event? The reason is because the bride is a mystery. Every parable of the Lord Jesus relating to weddings never give information about the bride; one only hears about the groom and the guests. All through successive ages and generations, the church of Christ, which is the bride of Christ, has always been kept as a mystery, a hidden secret. Most men don't speak about their beloved wives in public. A man's wife is his darling. He keeps matters about his darling wife to himself and to his chest; they are private to him. In the same vein, the Lord Jesus kept matters about His bride, the church, to Himself. This was a well-kept secret throughout the Old Testament, including during the earthly ministry of the Lord Jesus Himself. The church could not be revealed until three important things took place in the first instance: the gruesome death of Christ on the cross. His glorious resurrection; and the outpouring of the Holy Spirit on mankind, meaning the Holy Spirit had to leave heaven and come down to earth. The church is the result of all three things listed. So we can see how precious the church is to the Lord; the reason He kept her as a mystery all through the ages and generations as alluded to in the word of God, saying, "This message was kept secret for centuries and generations past, but now it has been revealed to God's people. For God wanted them to know that the riches and glory of Christ are for you Gentiles too. And this is the secret: *Christ lives in you*. This gives you assurance of sharing his glory" (Colossians 1:26–27 NLT). How amazing it is to know that "Christ lives in you" is a divine mystery, a secret surprise that has been concealed from the world for several centuries and generations. This divine mystery is a secret surprise that has been concealed from the world for generations (Colossians 1:26 TPT). The mystery that Christ lives in you is the biblical definition of a Christian, someone in whom Christ is alive and has taken His abode. If the mystery is Christ lives in you, according to Colossians 1:26, and Christ living in you is what it means to be a Christian, therefore one can safely conclude that the Christian has been the divine mystery of God all these centuries and generations. The church of Christ is made of a collection of Christians; therefore, the church of Christ is this divine mystery of God that has been concealed from the whole world for centuries and generations. This is mind-blowing. It shows how precious the church is to God. The church of Christ is the most glorious creation of God, excelling in glory, virtue, beauty, and power. Matters about the church could not be revealed to men until the Holy Spirit, the overseer of the church of Christ on earth, came down from heaven to earth to oversee the church. This is fully discussed in the next chapter, where the birth of the church is unveiled in yet another parable of the Lord Jesus Christ. It is worth noting that in the previous chapter, where the Parable of the Prodigal Son was discussed, Christ was kept as a great mystery in that parable. Similarly, in this parable of the wedding feast, we can see that the body of Christ, which is the church, has been kept as a great mystery as well. What an insightful observation! The invited guests in the parable are the many that are called; but the bride is the few that are chosen. Everyone invited to the feast is both a guest and a potential bride. A collection of all individuals that have been chosen as bride gives rise, collectively, to the bride. The bride is singular because it is a group or collection of individuals. Everyone is invited to the wedding feast as a guest, but in the end, those that are dressed in the correct attire for the feast will be taken in as the bride. In this parable, everyone present was a guest. A collection of all guests that had the correct attire make up the bride. The speechless man and other folks like him, who were not dressed in the correct attire for the feast, are rejected and thrown out into darkness. They are not chosen as part of the bride. The reason is because the bride is pure, holy, and undefiled as seen in Ephesians 5:25–27, which says, "Husbands, love your wives, just as Christ loved the church and gave himself up for her to make her holy, cleansing her by the washing with water through the word, and to present her to himself as a *radiant church, without stain or wrinkle or any other blemish, but holy and blameless."* Right now, everyone is in church as followers of Christ; however, many are doing their own thing, not heeding the words of Christ. On the day the Lord returns to take the bride home to heaven for the marriage supper of the Lamb, only true believers that have lived for the Lord, obeying His word and practicing righteousness, would go with Him. It doesn't matter what status a believer has in his local church; he may be a deacon, pastor, reverend, bishop, archbishop, elder, brother, sister, or a ministry leader. If not found worthy as a bride of Christ, he won't join in the wedding feast. That means he was only a guest and not a bride. The true bride of Christ, the true church, is radiant, holy, blameless, without stain, without wrinkle, and without blemish, as earlier seen in Ephesians 5:25–27. This is why the believer must remain focused and run his Christian race personally. Our personal, individual walk with the Lord Jesus will determine who is His bride and who is not. Therefore, take personal responsibility for walking faithfully, righteously, and holily with the Lord Jesus Christ.

> All who have this hope in him purify themselves, just as he is pure. (1 John 3:3)

Not everyone present in church wants to be the bride of Christ. Some want to remain as mere guests. They live for themselves and do whatever they like. They don't heed the word of God. But you must not live this way if you want to be the bride at the wedding feast. If you have the hope of being the bride at the wedding feast, then you must purify yourself, just as the Lord Jesus is pure.

## Summary

The Parable of the Wedding Feast has been unveiled in this chapter. The underlying message shows the wedding feast is the same as the marriage supper of the Lamb, which is recorded in Revelation 19:7–9. This is the wedding feast that will take place in heaven in the presence of the King of the universe, God the Father. The Lord Jesus Christ is the groom, and His church is the bride. The reason for this extravagant wedding feast, the type that has never been seen before, is seen in the Parable of the Prodigal Son, where the Father arranged a party to celebrate the return of his lost son back home. In the same vein, this wedding feast is to celebrate and consummate the return of mankind (both Jews and Gentiles) back to God through Christ. The Jews were the people originally invited for the wedding feast, but they rejected the invitation. Therefore, the invitation was extended to the whole world, comprising of both the good and bad, Jews and Gentiles. During the wedding feast, the Lord found a man that was present among the invited guests but didn't have his wedding robe of righteousness on him, signifying someone who associates as a member of the body of Christ but was not genuinely in Christ. The Lord asked him why this was so, but the man was speechless. The angels of God then came and bound him hand and foot and threw him out into outer darkness. Many, the whole world, are called to this wedding feast, but only few are chosen. It is observed that the parable has the groom and invited guests but no mention of the bride anywhere. It was discussed in this chapter that the reason why there is no mention of the bride is because the invited guests also double potentially as the bride, a collection of them. The many called are the invited guests. The few chosen are collectively the bride. All those that have been chosen as bride dress in the wedding robe provided for the wedding feast. Those without the provided wedding robe are thrown out into darkness. Therefore, every bride of Christ must stand holy and pure in Christ's righteousness alone and must abide in Him. We must abide and stay rooted in Christ. In the Parable of the Prodigal Son, earlier discussed in chapter 2, we saw the bringing of the Gentiles into the family of God, reconnecting them to the blessing of Abraham. In this chapter, where the Parable of the Wedding Feast has been discussed, it's seen that the wedding feast has both Jews and Gentiles, all of mankind, as invited guests. This brings us nicely to the Parable of the Good Samaritan in the next chapter, where all of mankind, comprising of both Jews and Gentiles, are reconciled back to God through the death and resurrection of the Lord Jesus Christ. In the Parable of the Good Samaritan, we also see the revelation and birth of the church, following the glorious arrival of the Holy Spirit, the overseer of the church of Christ here on earth. All of these are powerfully unveiled and discussed in the next chapter. The Parable of the Good Samaritan is an extraordinary parable. It is probably the parable with the most detailed account of Christ's work of salvation for all mankind.

# CHAPTER 4

# The Parable of the Good Samaritan (Luke 10:30–37)

Then Jesus answered and said: "A certain man went down from Jerusalem to Jericho, and fell among thieves, who stripped him of his clothing, wounded him, and departed, leaving him half dead. Now by chance a certain priest came down that road. And when he saw him, he passed by on the other side. Likewise a Levite, when he arrived at the place, came and looked, and passed by on the other side. But a certain Samaritan, as he journeyed, came where he was. And when he saw him, he had compassion. So he went to him and bandaged his wounds, pouring on oil and wine; and he set him on his own animal, brought him to an inn, and took care of him. On the next day, when he departed, he took out two denarii, gave them to the innkeeper, and said to him, 'Take care of him; and whatever more you spend, when I come again, I will repay you.' So which of these three do you think was neighbor to him who fell among the thieves?" And he said, "He who showed mercy on him." Then Jesus said to him, "Go and do likewise."

—Luke 10:30–37 NKJV

In chapter 2, we discussed the Parable of the Prodigal Son, where we saw the demonstration of extraordinary love and compassion by a merciful father. In this chapter, we are focusing on the Parable of the Good Samaritan, which is one of the most incredible parables told by our Lord Jesus Christ. The Parable of the Good Samaritan and the Parable of the Prodigal Son have very different surface stories but with very similar underlying messages. These two parables, I suppose, are the two most incredible parables told by our Lord Jesus Christ. It's amazing and equally awe-inspiring to see the extraordinary divine wisdom which was manifested in the Lord Jesus in the creation of these two parables, both of which, when combined, capture the full extent of God's work of salvation for all mankind.

As noted earlier in chapter 1, which is worth reiterating repeatedly, the Lord Jesus is the wisdom of God (1 Corinthians 1:24). He is the epitome of divine wisdom; He's wisdom personified. In Him is hidden and domiciled all the treasures of wisdom and knowledge (Colossians 2:3). When the Lord Jesus walked the earth, that was wisdom literally having hands and legs and walking the streets of Galilee. The Lord Jesus is the wisdom behind all of God's creation. God possessed this wisdom at the beginning of His works (Proverbs 8:22), and by Him all things were made, for nothing in the universe was made without Him (John 1:3). For by Him were all things created that are in heaven and that are in earth, visible and invisible, whether they be thrones or dominions or principalities or powers; all things were created by Him and for Him (Colossians 1:16). Indeed, what manner of man is Jesus! This same Jesus is the one we proclaim, admonishing and teaching everyone with all wisdom so that we may present everyone fully mature in Christ (Colossians 1:28).

The Parable of the Prodigal Son and the Parable of the Good Samaritan both demonstrate the extraordinary depth of God's love, mercy, and compassion for mankind. Thank God for the Jewish lawyer, who, "wanting to justify himself, said to Jesus, 'And who is my neighbor?'" (Luke 10:29 NKJV). It was while providing an answer to the Jewish lawyer's question about who was his neighbor that the Lord Jesus came up with this most incredible parable in the whole Bible. Had the lawyer not asked the question about who his neighbor was, the Lord Jesus wouldn't have had the need to tell this parable, and we would never have known this incredible story or the powerful underlying message that it carries for all mankind.

## Unveiling the Parable of the Good Samaritan

This is an extraordinary, interesting parable given by our Lord Jesus Christ. Let's begin to unveil the parable in chronological order, from verse to verse, for full understanding of the underlying message:

1. *"A certain man"*: "And Jesus answering said, a certain man went down from Jerusalem to Jericho" (vs 30). To unveil the certain man in this parable, we must first look at the originating place for his journey. This certain man started his journey from Jerusalem, which is the spiritual headquarters of God here on earth. Jerusalem is very significant in the agenda of God. In short, all Abrahamic religions revere Jerusalem as a sacred and holy city. Our Lord Jesus Christ was crucified and buried in Jerusalem. Following His resurrection, He first appeared to His disciples in Jerusalem. He instructed His disciples to tarry in Jerusalem until the Holy Spirit is sent by the Father. The disciples were instructed to preach the gospel starting in Jerusalem (Acts 1:8). When the Antichrist is revealed during the great tribulation, he will sit in the temple in Jerusalem and defile it (Daniel 9:27). When the Lord Jesus Christ returns, during the millennial reign of Christ, He will sit in the temple in Jerusalem and rule the whole earth from there. At the end of the age, when everything is done away with, and the current earth is passed away, the new earth that will unfold from heaven will be called the new Jerusalem.

   > Then I saw "a new heaven and a new earth," for the first heaven and the first earth had passed away, and there was no longer any sea. I saw the Holy City, the new Jerusalem, coming down out of heaven from God, prepared as a bride

beautifully dressed for her husband. (Revelation 21:1–2)

The reason why the new earth will be called the new Jerusalem is because the old earth (old Jerusalem), which is the current earth, was originally made as Jerusalem. Against this backdrop, we can see that Jerusalem in this parable symbolizes the current earth or, precisely, the garden of Eden when man was originally created. This is the place where God put the man He created (Genesis 2:8, 15). The certain man symbolizes Adam, the first man made by God. He stands here, representing all of mankind. The name Adam means man or mankind, made from the earth (ground) (Genesis 1:26, 27; 2:15–25). So this is Adam or mankind exploring the earth from the garden of Eden (Jerusalem) and then fell among thieves, which then brings us to the second character in the parable, the thieves.

2. *"The thieves"*: "…and fell among thieves" (vs 30). The thief has been identified for us in Scripture by our Lord Jesus Christ, when He said, "The thief comes only to steal and kill and destroy" (John 10:10). The apostle Peter, in his epistle, identified this thief as a devourer, saying, "Be sober, be vigilant; because your adversary the devil, as a roaring lion, walketh about, seeking whom he may devour" (1 Peter 5:8). The thief is further identified by the Lord Jesus Christ when unveiling the Parable of the Sower.

> When anyone hears the message about the kingdom and does not understand it, the *evil one* comes and snatches away what was sown in their heart. This is the seed sown along the path. (Matthew 13:19)

The thief is the evil one; that is the devil. He's the one that comes to steal, kill, and destroy, which is his mission statement. This was exactly what he did to Adam, representing mankind. Adam, as he journeyed on earth from the garden of Eden, was attacked by "thieves," which symbolize the devil and his demonic agents. From this parable, the Lord Jesus Christ gives us one vital information that's not captured in the Genesis account of the fall of man: Adam was attacked by thieves, meaning more than one thief. This shows that the plan to attack Adam, using the weapons of deception and sin, was planned and orchestrated by the devil and his demonic agents (other fallen angels, known as demons). Although this plan was executed by the devil himself, but it was planned by him and his demons. We see a similar situation in the Parable of the Sower, when it says, "As he was scattering the seed, some fell along the path, and the *birds* came and ate it up" (Matthew 13:4). While the parable has the birds in plural, meaning more than one bird, however, in the interpretation, the Lord Jesus referred to the birds as the evil one, which is singular. This shows that the Lord is referring to the birds collectively as one person, the devil, after all, it's the spirit of the devil that's at work in all of them. In the same vein, although Adam was attacked by thieves, but because they are one and the same, they can collectively be referred to as one person, the devil, which is what has been done in the account given in Genesis. It is important to note that the phrase "*fell* among thieves" indicates that Adam fell into the sin that was projected toward him by the devil. That was how the devil attacked him; sin was the devil's weapon of attack, and Adam fell into it. So we've seen that the thieves in this parable symbolize the devil.

3. *"He was stripped of his clothing, wounded, and left half dead"*: "Who stripped him of his clothing, wounded him, and departed, leaving him half dead" (vs 30). This is so remarkable. What happened here is the whole reason why the Lord Jesus Christ came from heaven to save mankind. When this man was attacked, the only thing the thieves took from him was his clothes. This shows that his clothes were very precious and enviable. This is the history of the best robe in the Parable of the Prodigal Son already explained in previous chapters. The best robe came about because this man was stripped of his clothes. The stripped clothes here symbolize Adamic authority, power, dominion, and glory, which man had

before the fall. God gave man dominion over the whole earth and everything in it (Genesis 1:26). He then crowned him with glory and honor, as expressed by the psalmist, saying, "What is man that You are mindful of him, And the son of man that You visit him? For You have made him a little lower than the angels, And You have crowned him with glory and honor. You have made him to have dominion over the works of Your hands; You have put all things under his feet" (Psalm 8:4–6 NKJV). This Adamic dominion and authority are what the devil stripped man of using the weapon of sin. He stole it, the reason he's known as the thief. He left man half dead. Man, comprising of both the spirit and the physical, became spiritually dead and was only alive physically. Man was eternally separated from God and fell from grace. He was severely wounded by sin, orchestrated by the devil. Mankind was wounded beyond repair. Man, in his wounded state, became a deviation from the original intent and purpose of God, his Creator. When God originally made man, he was made in the image and likeness of God, as expressed in Genesis 5:1–2, saying, "When God created mankind, he made them in the likeness of God. He created them male and female and blessed them. And he named them 'Mankind' when they were created." However, when the devil attacked him with sin, and he fell from grace, he bore a different image from what God originally created—the Adamic image, which is a fallen image, an image of sin. It was this wounded image that Adam passed down to his descendants through his son Seth, which Genesis 5:3 records as, "When Adam had lived 130 years, he had a son in his own likeness, in his own image; and he named him Seth." Adam had already fallen from grace before giving birth to Seth, who became the forefather of Noah (Genesis 5:1–28). The image he passed down to Seth is the image of sin, of the fallen mankind. Mankind was terribly wounded by sin. When God destroyed the world by flood, only Noah and his family survived. Therefore, the world that followed after the flood came from Noah, who already inherited the fallen image of sin from Seth. This is the full story of the fall of mankind, as powerfully expressed by the Lord Jesus Himself through this incredible parable.

4. *"A certain priest"*: "Now by chance a certain priest came down that road. And when he saw him, he passed by on the other side" (vs 31). From John 1:17, we understand that the law was given by Moses, but grace and truth came by Jesus Christ. The certain priest symbolizes the law given by Moses. The law of Moses could not help the badly wounded mankind. Moses came with the law to try and help this man, but the law was weak and useless to the plight of the wounded mankind. Speaking about the law of Moses, Romans 8:3–4 says, "For what the law was powerless to do because it was weakened by the flesh, God did by sending his own Son in the likeness of sinful flesh to be a sin offering. And so he condemned sin in the flesh, in order that the righteous requirement of the law might be fully met in us, who do not live according to the flesh but according to the Spirit." The law was weak and powerless and couldn't help this wounded mankind. The Scriptures further revealed that although the law was weak and powerless, it was also weak and useless, as expressed in Hebrews 7:18–19, which says, "The former regulation is set aside because it was weak and useless (for the law made nothing perfect), and a better hope is introduced, by which we draw near to God." It is therefore clear that the law of Moses, which is the certain priest, had no capacity to help this wounded man. The law was weak, powerless, and useless. It had no ability or capacity to help this wounded man. It is important to note that the certain priest came along that road by chance, meaning his journey wasn't originally planned or intended. That means the law came by chance; it wasn't God's original plan for mankind, neither was it God's perfect will for mankind. It came by Moses, according to Scriptures, and was weak, powerless, and useless. It can therefore be seen that the certain priest couldn't help the wounded mankind because he was weak, powerless, and useless. He was helpless himself, so he was of no help to the wounded mankind.

5. *"A Levite"*: "Likewise a Levite, when he arrived at the place, came and looked, and passed by on the other side" (vs 32). The phrase "likewise a Levite" means, like the certain priest, the Levite also came there by chance. While speaking to Moses in Exodus, God referred to Aaron, Moses's brother, as a *Levite*, and He appointed him to be Moses's prophet and mouthpiece: "Then the Lord's anger burned against Moses and he said, 'What about your brother, Aaron the Levite? I know he can speak well. He is already on his way to meet you, and he will be glad to see you.'" (Exodus 4:14). "Then the Lord said to Moses, 'See, I have made you like God to Pharaoh, and your brother Aaron will be your prophet.'" (Exodus 7:1). The Levites are God's servants, the prophets. The Levite in this parable symbolizes the prophets. Both the law, symbolized by the certain priest, and the prophets, symbolized by the Levite, preceded the coming of Christ. This is what Luke 16:16 says, "The Law and the Prophets were proclaimed until John. Since that time, the good news of the kingdom of God is being preached, and everyone is forcing their way into it."

> For all the Prophets and the Law prophesied until John. (Matthew 11:13)

We earlier discussed that the law was powerless in helping mankind. When the law, certain priest, came to the scene where the wounded man was lying half dead, he was useless as he couldn't help this wounded man in any way. When he saw the wounded man, he passed by on the other side. He made no attempt at trying to help this man because he himself was weak and useless in rendering any form of help. He had no capacity to help mankind. On the contrary, in the case of the prophets, symbolized by the Levite, we see that "when he arrived at the place, came and looked, and passed by on the other side" (Luke 10:32). The Levite went closer to have a look at the wounded man before crossing to the other side of the road. He at least tried something that the certain priest didn't do. This shows that the prophets came closer to helping the wounded mankind than the law, which was very far away from being able to help mankind. The prophets here is symbolized by Elijah, who stands to represent all the Old Testament prophets. We can as well place John the Baptist in the place of Elijah, as we know from Scriptures that he, John the Baptist, came in the spirit and power of Elijah.

> He will bring back many of the people of Israel to the Lord their God. And he will go on before the Lord, in the spirit and power of Elijah, to turn the hearts of the parents to their children and the disobedient to the wisdom of the righteous—to make ready a people prepared for the Lord. (Luke 1:16–17)

Accordingly, John the Baptist, standing in the place of Elijah, representing all Old Testament prophets, came very close to the salvation of mankind. From Luke 1:16–17, we can see that John the Baptist brought back many children of Israel to God. He turned the hearts of the parents to their children. He turned the disobedient to the wisdom of the righteous. He made ready a people prepared for the Lord. By virtue of this task undertaken by John the Baptist, the prophets exceeded the works done by the law. The law was weak and useless, but the prophets prepared the way for the Messiah. In fact, it was John the Baptist, representing the prophets, that baptized the Lord Jesus (Matthew 3:13) and correctly identified Him to the people as the Lamb of God that takes away the sins of the whole world:

> The next day John saw Jesus coming toward him and said, "Look, the Lamb of God, who takes away the sin of the world! This is the one I meant when I said, 'A man who comes after me has surpassed me because he was before me.' I myself did not know him, but the reason 'I came baptizing with water' was that he might be revealed to Israel." Then John gave this testimony: "I saw the Spirit come down from heaven as a dove and remain on him. And I myself did not know him,

but the one who sent me to baptize with water told me, 'The man on whom you see the Spirit come down and remain is the one who will baptize with the Holy Spirit.' I have seen and I testify that this is God's Chosen One." (John 1:29–34)

By virtue of John the Baptist baptizing the Lord Jesus and identifying Him to the people, he did something that was eternally greater than all the law ever did. This is why in the parable, the Levite, when he arrived at the place, came and looked. The certain priest couldn't come close to look at the wounded man, but the Levite did, signifying that the prophets came much closer to helping mankind than the law ever did. This is so profound and accurately captured in the underlying message of this powerful parable delivered by our Lord Jesus Christ. It is important to note that the Levite came along that road by chance, the same as the certain priest, meaning his journey wasn't originally planned or intended. That means the prophets came by chance; they weren't God's original plan for mankind. Although the prophets couldn't help mankind, as has already been discussed, however they came closer to helping the wounded mankind than the law.

6. *"A certain Samaritan"*: "But a certain Samaritan, as he journeyed, came where he was. And when he saw him, he had compassion" (vs 33). The Samaritans in the day of this parable were greatly despised by the Jews. They were seen as unclean, like pigs. The Jews had no regard or respect for them. In fact, to the Jews, there was nothing beautiful or majestic about Samaritans. The prophet Isaiah describes the lowly state and unattractive appearance of this Samaritan by saying, "Who has believed our message and to whom has the arm of the Lord been revealed? He grew up before him like a tender shoot, and like a root out of dry ground. He had no beauty or majesty to attract us to him, nothing in his appearance that we should desire him. He was despised and rejected by mankind, a man of suffering, and familiar with pain. Like one from whom people hide their faces he was despised, and we held him in low esteem" (Isaiah 53:1–3). This is not just

a good Samaritan; this is the Lord Jesus Christ Himself. The certain Samaritan in this parable symbolizes the Lord Jesus Christ Himself. He came to the world like a Samaritan, even though He was God. He was despised of men. This is still a huge mystery to the Jews and many around the world today. Many still think the Lord Jesus was a prophet or a great religious leader, not knowing He was the incarnated Word of the living God Himself, being God in human flesh. The apostle Paul, writing by the Spirit, says, "You must have the same attitude that Christ Jesus had. Though *he was God,* he did not think of equality with God as something to cling to. Instead, he gave up his divine privileges; he took the humble position of a slave and was born as a human being. When he appeared in human form, he humbled himself in obedience to God and died a criminal's death on a cross" (Philippians 2:5–8 NLT). The people expected Him to come in His full regalia as God or monarch of the universe, but He decided to show up as a mere Samaritan. He was even born in a manger (Luke 2:7). The apostle John, writing by the Spirit, succinctly captures this in the gospel, saying, "He was in the world, and the world was made by him, and the world knew him not. He came unto his own, and his own received him not. But as many as received him, to them gave he power to become the sons of God, even to them that believe on his name" (John 1:10–12 KJV). His own couldn't recognize Him because He came as a Samaritan. He was despised and rejected by mankind because He came as a Samaritan. They didn't recognize Him to know, by faith and spiritual discernment, that this was the incarnated word of God, who was from the beginning (John 1:1–2). The Jews despitefully referred to Him as a Samaritan out of their disdain for Him and His ministry (John 8:48). The Lord Jesus Christ is the Good Samaritan. He is the Good Master (Matthew 19:16), the good shepherd that lays down His life for His flock (John 10:11), the One anointed by God with the Holy Ghost and with power, who went about doing good and healing all that were oppressed of the devil, for God was with Him (Acts 10:38). It is worth highlighting an important point from this verse 33, which is captured in the phrase "he had compassion." Here we see the same attribute of compassion exhibited by Father God in the Parable of the Prodigal Son earlier discussed in chapter 2. Like God the Father showed mercy and compassion on the prodigal son, here we see God the Son, showing the same love, mercy, and compassion on mankind. What a God of mercy and compassion we serve! In both parables of the prodigal son and Good Samaritan, we see the extraordinary demonstration of God's love, mercy, and compassion to mankind. No wonder John 3:16 says, "For God so loved the world that he gave his one and only Son, that whoever believes in him shall not perish but have eternal life." Romans 5:8 further says, "But God demonstrates his own love for us in this: While we were still sinners, Christ died for us." Jesus Christ is our Good Samaritan. The priest and the Levite preceded the Good Samaritan in the same way the law and the prophets preceded Christ.

> The Law and the Prophets were proclaimed until John. Since that time, the good news of the kingdom of God is being preached, and everyone is forcing their way into it. (Luke 16:16)

Interestingly, before the Lord Jesus Christ went to the cross to save mankind, Moses and Elijah, representing the law and the prophets, appeared and spoke with Him on the mount of transfiguration. What we see here is the certain priest and Levite came down to the Good Samaritan when he was about to treat the badly wounded man, bandaging him and pouring oil and wine on his wounds. Although we don't have the benefit of knowing what they discussed with him, but it is certainly related to what needed to be done to treat the wounded man. The Lord's death on the cross was what He used in treating the wounds and pains of mankind, and it's that same death that both Moses and Elijah came to speak to the Lord Jesus about. This is what the Bible says:

> Then two men appeared and began talking with him—Moses and Elijah! They were splendid in appearance, glorious to see; and they were

speaking of his death at Jerusalem, to be carried out in accordance with God's plan. (Luke 9:30–31 TLB)

7. *"A certain Samaritan, as he journeyed"*: "A certain Samaritan, as he journeyed, came where he was" (vs 33): The Lord Jesus gave an extremely vital information from the phrase "as he journeyed". This is so profound! Let's carefully observe here that the Good Samaritan came across the wounded man while on his planned journey along that road, unlike the certain priest and Levite, who, according to the parable, came across the wounded man as they journeyed on that road by chance. The priest came to the scene of the wounded man by accident. His journey through that road was not originally planned or intended. This shows that the law of Moses came by accident. It was not in God's original plan and purpose for the salvation of mankind. Like the priest, the Levite, which symbolizes the prophets, also came to that road by chance: "Likewise a Levite…" This too wasn't God's original plan or purpose for the salvation of mankind. But the Good Samaritan, which symbolizes our Lord Jesus Christ, the good shepherd, came to that road while undertaking His own planned journey: "But a certain Samaritan, *as he journeyed*, came where he was." This shows that in line with God's word, the Lord Jesus Christ planned His journey of salvation for mankind. The work of salvation has been God's plan and purpose since the foundation of the world. It didn't come by accident. It didn't happen as an afterthought. This was God's plan for mankind all the while, even before the creation and subsequent fall of Adam. We can see that the Good Samaritan (Our Lord and Savior, Jesus Christ) carefully planned His journey through that same road for Him to rescue the certain man (mankind) that was bound to fall into the hands of the thieves (Satan and his demons). So God knew all the while that Adam would fall and fail, and He already made a way of escape for him before the foundation of the earth through His Son, Jesus Christ. The divine plan of God for the salvation of mankind was perfected and realized

through the death and resurrection of our Lord Jesus Christ. The Scriptures let us know that the Lamb was slain for the salvation of mankind from the foundation of the world, as expressed in Revelation13:8 (KJV): "...the Lamb slain from the foundation of the world." Furthermore, Ephesians 2:10 (KJV) says, "For we are His workmanship, created in Christ Jesus for good works, which God prepared beforehand that we should walk in them." The Lord Jesus Christ, according to 1 Peter 1:20 (KJV), was foreordained before the foundation of the world, but was manifest in these last times for you." Before the beginning of time, the Lord Jesus had already purposed or planned to save mankind, according to 2 Timothy 1:9 (KJV), which says, "Who has saved us and called us with a holy calling, not according to our works, but according to His own purpose and grace which was given to us in Christ Jesus before time began." The Lord's journey to save mankind was carefully planned and executed. It was not an accident. It was not an afterthought. It was God's ultimate plan for the rescue and salvation of all mankind.

8. *"He bandaged his wounds, pouring on oil and wine"*: "So he went to him and bandaged his wounds, pouring on oil and wine" (vs 34). This symbolizes the magnificent work of Christ on the cross. It was on the cross that the Lord Jesus Christ paid in full for the sin of all mankind. The Lord Jesus died on the cross, destroying the power of sin and death over mankind. The Lord Jesus took care of the sin of mankind once and for all, according to Romans 8:3–4, which says, "For what the law was powerless to do because it was weakened by the flesh, God did by sending his own Son in the likeness of sinful flesh to be a sin offering. And so he condemned sin in the flesh, in order that the righteous requirement of the law might be fully met in us, who do not live according to the flesh but according to the Spirit." The prophet Isaiah, writing this prophetically about seven hundred years before Christ, said, "But he was pierced for our transgressions, he was crushed for our iniquities; the punishment that brought us peace was on him, and by his wounds we are healed. We all, like sheep, have gone astray, each of us has turned to

our own way; and the Lord has laid on him the iniquity of us all" (Isaiah 53:5–6). The Lord Jesus treated the wounded man using His own blood and life. This is what pouring on oil and wine symbolize. Oil is a prophetic symbol for the anointing, which is the Holy Spirit, as found in Isaiah 61:1 and Luke 4:18, which say, "The Spirit of the Lord God is upon me because He's anointed me…" Although the oil symbolizes the Holy Spirit, however, the Bible also indicates that the Holy Spirit is symbolized by water, according to the words of the Lord Jesus, when He said, "'Whoever believes in me, as Scripture has said, rivers of living water will flow from within them.' By this he meant the Spirit, whom those who believed in him were later to receive. Up to that time the Spirit had not been given since Jesus had not yet been glorified" (John 7:38–39). Here we see that water is also a prophetic symbol for the Holy Spirit. That therefore means that both oil and water are prophetic symbols for the Holy Spirit. We can safely conclude that both oil and water are the same prophetically. In that sense, it can therefore be said that the oil that the Good Samaritan poured on the wounds of the wounded man is a prophetic symbol for water and the Holy Spirit. Similarly, wine was also poured on the wounds of the wounded man. As we generally know, wine symbolizes the blood, and this is widely known from the Holy Communion wine, where the wine symbolizes the blood of our Lord Jesus Christ, according to Matthew 26:27–28, which says, "Then he took a cup, and when he had given thanks, he gave it to them, saying, 'Drink from it, all of you. This is my blood of the covenant, which is poured out for many for the forgiveness of sins.'" On this basis, it can therefore be seen that the oil and wine that were poured on the wounded man's wounds prophetically represent water and blood. This was exactly what the Lord Jesus Christ poured out on the cross for the remission of the sin of mankind. The earlier scripture above says, "This is my blood of the covenant, which is poured out for many for the forgiveness of sins" (Matthew 26:28). This was fulfilled when the lifeless body of the Lord Jesus was hanging on the cross, and a Roman soldier came to pierce his side with a spear.

John 19:33–34 says, "But when they came to Jesus and found that he was already dead, they did not break his legs. Instead, one of the soldiers pierced Jesus' side with a spear, bringing a sudden flow of blood and water." This was where the Lord Jesus poured out blood and water, which are symbolized by the wine and oil in the parable, for the salvation of mankind. The blood is His life, which has been poured out for mankind and has made eternal life available to everyone that believes. The water is the outpouring of His Holy Spirit to all mankind, to as many that would believe in Him, in fulfillment of the word of God, given prophetically by the prophet Joel, when he said, "And afterward, I will pour out my Spirit on all people. Your sons and daughters will prophesy, your old men will dream dreams, your young men will see visions. Even on my servants, both men and women, I will pour out my Spirit in those days" (Joel 2:28–29). From the Bible, we understand that this prophecy was fulfilled on the day of Pentecost, according to the apostle Peter, when by the Holy Spirit, he said, "These people are not drunk, as you suppose. It's only nine in the morning! No, this is what was spoken by the prophet Joel: 'In the last days, God says, I will pour out my Spirit on all people. Your sons and daughters will prophesy, your young men will see visions, your old men will dream dreams. Even on my servants, both men and women, I will pour out my Spirit in those days, and they will prophesy'" (Acts 2:15–18). Had the Lord Jesus not poured out blood and water from His pierced side, the overflow of His life and Holy Spirit would not have been possible. He used the blood (eternal life) and water (Holy Spirit) to cure the sin of mankind, resulting in the remission of the sin of mankind. This is the exact scenario that played out in the parable with the use of oil (water) and wine (blood) in the treatment of the wounded man. Interestingly, the prophet Hosea, by the spirit of God, gave out this vital information prophetically when he proclaimed, "'It shall come to pass in that day that I will answer,' says the Lord; 'I will answer the heavens, and they shall answer the earth. The earth shall answer with *grain*, with new *wine*, and with *oil*; they shall answer Jezreel. Then I will sow her for Myself in the earth, and I will have mercy on her who had not obtained mercy; then I will say to those who were not My people, You are My people! And they shall say, You are my God!'" (Hosea 2:21–23). The grain in this prophetic passage symbolizes the body of the Lord Jesus Christ, the living bread, which was broken for the salvation of mankind. The flour from which bread is made comes from grain. The bread is the broken body of the Lord (Matthew 26:26). The wine and oil symbolize the Lord's blood and Holy Spirit, already explained. The grain, wine, and oil were used for the reconciliation of mankind back to God, and these three, according 1 John 5:8, also bear witness here on earth and agree as one.

> And there are three that bear witness on earth: the Spirit, the water, and the blood; and these three agree as one. (1 John 5:8 NKJV)

The water here symbolizes the word of God (Ephesians 5:26), which is the Bread of Life (John 6:35).

9. *"He set him on his own animal (beast)"* (vs 34): Some other Bible translations use *beast* or *donkey* in place of *animal* in the phrase "he set him on his own animal"; however, the key words here are "his own." "His own donkey or beast or animal" symbolizes his own body. The Good Samaritan carried the wounded man in his own beast. This was how the Lord Jesus bore the griefs and carried the sorrow of mankind. The apostle Peter, writing on this, said, "Who *his own self* bare our sins in *his own body* on the tree, that we, being dead to sins, should live unto righteousness: by whose stripes ye were healed" (1 Peter 2:24 KJV). The wounded man was carried by the Lord in His own body, "that it might be fulfilled which was spoken by Esaias the prophet, saying, *Himself took our infirmities*, and *bare our sicknesses*" (Matthew 8:17 KJV). This is the reason we break bread, signifying the Lord's body that was broken for us when He died for the sin of all mankind. He carried mankind in His own body, which was bro-

ken for our sake that we should be made whole. Isaiah, writing, said, "Surely he hath borne our griefs, and carried our sorrows: yet we did esteem him stricken, smitten of God, and afflicted. But he was wounded for our transgressions, he was bruised for our iniquities: the chastisement of our peace was upon him; and with his stripes we are healed" (Isaiah 53:4–5 KJV). The Lord demonstrated this in the breaking of bread, when "he took bread, gave thanks and broke it, and gave it to them, saying, 'This is my body given for you; do this in remembrance of me'" (Luke 22:19). While on the cross, the Lord Jesus bore the sin of mankind. He became the sacrificial lamb that took away the sin of all mankind (John 1:29). God made the Lord Jesus sin, who knew no sin, so that we might become the righteousness of God in Him (2 Corinthians 5:21). The Lord carried your sin, and my sin in His own body.

10. *"He brought him to an inn and took care of him"* (vs 34): This symbolizes the carrying of the wounded man to church to be revived or cared for. The inn symbolizes the church, which, like a hospital, is the place where the wounded man, who's now been rescued by the Lord Jesus, is being treated and revived. The Lord Jesus said, "It is not the healthy who need a doctor, but the sick" (Matthew 9:12). So the sick mankind is in dire need of Doctor Jesus Christ, the greatest physician there is, and the place He treats mankind is called the church, also known as the body of Christ. The medicine for treating the rescued man in church is the living word of God, which, according to Proverbs 4:22 (NLT), is medicine that "bring life to those who find them, and healing to their whole body." The innkeeper symbolizes the Holy Spirit, who is the managing director and chief executive of the church of Jesus Christ here on earth. He is the great Comforter and helper of the church of Christ on earth today. The carrying of the wounded man to the inn signifies the birth of the church of Christ, which is akin to a hospital, where mankind is being treated through the living word of God and the ministry of the Holy Spirit until the redeemed or rescued man becomes a fully grown, mature man in Christ Jesus. This is why the body of

Christ is equipped with different kinds of spiritual gifts, all for the building and edification of this redeemed man. This is what the Bible says:

> So Christ himself gave the apostles, the prophets, the evangelists, the pastors and teachers, to equip his people for works of service, so that the body of Christ may be built up until we all reach unity in the faith and in the knowledge of the Son of God and become mature, attaining to the whole measure of the fullness of Christ. (Ephesians 4:11–13)

This is the reason why the apostle Paul, by the Holy Spirit, said, "My dear children, for whom I am again in the pains of childbirth until Christ is formed in you" (Galatians 4:19). The redeemed man will go through a process of building and spiritual conditioning "until we all reach unity in the faith and in the knowledge of the Son of God and become mature, attaining to the whole measure of the fullness of Christ" (Ephesians 4:13). This is when it can be said that Christ has been formed in the life of an individual. This is the will of God for all His children. He doesn't want us to remain as infants, "tossed back and forth by the waves, and blown here and there by every wind of teaching and by the cunning and craftiness of people in their deceitful scheming" (Ephesians 4:14). The major platform that God has designed for bringing the redeemed man to the full stature of Christ is the word of God. The importance of the word of God to the redeemed can never be overemphasized. This is why Acts 20:32 says, "Now I commit you to God and to the word of his grace, which can build you up and give you an inheritance among all those who are sanctified." The word of God can build the believer and deliver to him all his inheritance in Christ Jesus. The word of God is the greatest platform by which God blesses His people. Always feed on the word of God. It is food for the soul of mankind, especially the redeemed man.

11. *"He took out two denarii and gave to the innkeeper"*: "On the next day, when he departed, he took out two denarii, gave them to the innkeeper, and said to him, 'Take care of him; and whatever more you spend, when I come again, I will repay you'" (vs 35). The Good Samaritan got the wounded man to the inn and paid two denarii as down payment for his treatment. One denarius was the typical daily wage of a worker at the time of this parable. That means the down payment of two denarii was for two days' wages. The Lord Jesus gave out this information in yet another parable, when He said, "For the kingdom of heaven is like a landowner who went out early in the morning to hire workers for his vineyard. He agreed to pay them a denarius for the day and sent them into his vineyard" (Matthew 22:1–2). Denarii is the plural of denarius. The payment of two denarii to the innkeeper denotes the down payment of two day's wages, which is fully captured in the italicized portion in the rendering given in the Amplified Classic version, which says, "And the next day he took out two denarii [*two day's wages*] and gave [them] to the innkeeper, saying, Take care of him; and whatever more you spend, I [myself] will repay you when I return" (Luke 10:35 AMPC). As has already been stated, the innkeeper symbolizes the Holy Spirit, who is the great Comforter, helper, and chief overseer of the church of Jesus Christ here on earth (John 16:16–17). So a down payment of two day's wages was made for the innkeeper to look after the redeemed man that's being revived. From scripture, we understand that "a thousand years in your sight are like a day that has just gone by, or like a watch in the night" (Psalm 90:4 KJV). Similarly, the apostle Peter, writing about this, said, "But, beloved, be not ignorant of this one thing, that one day is with the Lord as a thousand years, and a thousand years as one day" (2 Peter 3:8 KJV). It can therefore be seen from these two scriptures that one day is a prophetic symbol for one thousand years. Therefore, the two days down payment that was made by the Lord Jesus is a prophetic symbol for two thousand years. This therefore means that the Holy Spirit will look after the church on earth for two thousand years, and then

the Lord Jesus will return for His millennial reign on earth. This prophetic symbolism was also captured by the prophet Hosea, who lived more than seven hundred and fifty years before the Lord Jesus was born, when he said, "After two days he will revive us; on the third day he will restore us, that we may live in his presence" (Hosea 6:2). From these prophetic declarations of the Spirit, through the prophet Hosea, we can see that the church will spend two days (two thousand years) to be revived here on earth. Then on the third day (another one thousand years), the church will spend the millennial reign with the Lord Jesus Christ, reigning here on earth (Revelation 20:1–6). Thereafter, we will be in His presence forever and ever in the Holy City, the new Jerusalem (Revelation 21:2). It therefore means that the dispensation of the church is for two thousand years. That is, the wounded man is to be revived in the inn for two prophetic days or two thousand calendar years, starting from the day he was brought into the inn. Although the church was born when the Lord Jesus resurrected, however, it was on the day of Pentecost, which is fifty days from the day of Christ's resurrection that the church came alive and was officially commissioned.

12. *"Whatever more you spend and when I come again"*: "And whatever more you spend, when I come again, I will repay you" (vs 35). There are two points to be noted from this statement. The first is "whatever more you spend." This throws open the possibility for the church to remain longer than the two thousand years that's been prophetically declared as the dispensation of the church. This possibility has also been observed in yet another parable of the Lord, which is discussed in the next chapter of this book. Both scenarios indicate that there's a strong possibility for the church to still be around for a little longer than two thousand years. Unofficially, the church was born when Christ resurrected from the dead, as He is the head of the church; however, the church came alive and was officially born on the day of Pentecost, when the Holy Spirit was poured out. It was not possible for the inn to be operational when the innkeeper hasn't yet arrived. Although the inn was there, but until the innkeeper

arrived, the inn wasn't operational. This is the reason why it's mostly regarded that the church was born on the day of Pentecost, the day the Holy Spirit (innkeeper) officially touched down on earth to oversee the church of Christ. If two thousand is added to the year that the day of Pentecost happened, one would be so surprised to find out that the church is nearly there already. The time left for the church to fully complete its down payment of two thousand years is extremely short. The time is far spent, the Master is returning soon, as He promised when He said, "When I come again, I will repay you" (vs 35). The Lord Jesus Christ is coming back soon. We must get ready and be prepared.

> Therefore keep watch, because you do not know on what day your Lord will come. (Matthew 24:42)

We must remain watchful, prayerful, and careful at all times so that we don't get entangled with the affairs of this world, forgetting that the return of our Lord and Master is upon us. That was what happened to the five foolish virgins in the Parable of the Ten Virgins, which is discussed in detail in the next chapter. The five foolish virgins were not prepared and therefore missed the Lord's return. Therefore, you must "be careful, or your hearts will be weighed down with carousing, drunkenness and the anxieties of life, and that day will close on you suddenly like a trap. For it will come on all those who live on the face of the whole earth. Be always on the watch, and pray that you may be able to escape all that is about to happen, and that you may be able to stand before the Son of Man" (Luke 21:34–36).

## The birds, the thieves, and the enemy—the threefold ministry of the devil

In the Parable of the Sower, the devil manifested himself as the birds that came to eat up the seed that fell along the path, snatching away the seed of God's word that was sown in the heart of men. In this case, the devil can be seen to be a snatcher and a thief. In the Parable of the Weeds in the Field, the devil manifested himself as the enemy that came by night to sow weeds among the wheat. In this case, the devil can be seen to be a spoiler, a destroyer, whose intention was to spoil or destroy the wheats by corrupting it with weeds. In the Parable of the Good Samaritan, we see the same devil manifesting himself as the thieves that attacked and wounded mankind, stealing his garment, and leaving him half dead. Here the devil can be seen to be a violent attacker, a thief, and a murderer. The Lord Jesus let us know in John 8:44 that the devil has been "a murderer from the beginning, not holding to the truth, for there is no truth in him. When he lies, he speaks his native language, for he is a liar and the father of lies." These three different manifestations of the devil that have been highlighted in these parables reveal his threefold ministry of stealing, killing, and destroying, as has been identified in John 10:10 by the Lord Jesus Christ, when He said, "The thief comes only to steal and kill and destroy; I have come that they may have life, and have it to the full." These three are the mission statement of the devil. He's a devourer, who goes about aimlessly, seeking whom he might devour.

> Be alert and of sober mind. Your enemy the devil prowls around like a roaring lion looking for someone to devour. (1 Peter 5:8)

The devil stole Adam's garment and murdered him spiritually through sin. That's what he's still doing today: stealing, killing, and destroying destinies. As a child of God, you are far more superior to the devil. You must not be afraid of him as he has no power over you. Our Lord Jesus Christ has stripped him of his stolen power and authority. The Lord openly disarmed him. The Lord Jesus Christ victoriously triumphed over the devil and his demons, stripping them of their stolen Adamic powers. As a believer in Christ, you must know and be aware that Satan has been disgracefully defeated by the Lord Jesus Christ through the cross. You must now arise and walk in this victory that the Lord Jesus Christ has already won. This therefore brings us to the Adamic garment that was stolen from Adam when he was attacked.

## The stolen Adamic garment

The first thing that Satan did to Adam when he attacked him was to strip him of his garment. The stolen Adamic garment, which Adam had before the fall of mankind, is superior to the garment of sin and self-righteousness, a filthy rag, according to Isaiah 64:6, which is being worn by any man that's not in Christ Jesus. This is the garment of the fallen man. Since Satan got his power and illegal authority from the stolen Adamic garment, he therefore has superior power over men that are not in Christ Jesus, oppressing and subjugating them through the stolen Adamic power and authority. That was the same power used by the devil to oppress all of mankind before the Lord Jesus Christ came to save mankind by destroying the works of the devil (1 John 3:8). However, this Adamic garment, which Adam had before the fall of mankind, is inferior to the best robe and ring, which have been received by any man that's in Christ Jesus. The best robe and ring represent the righteousness, life, power, and authority that are available in Christ Jesus. This is the same as the life and righteousness of God Himself. It is the ultimate righteousness, life, power, and authority through Christ Jesus our Lord. Before the fall of mankind, Adam didn't have the righteousness of God; he didn't have the life (*zoe*) of God; he didn't have the fullness of the Spirit (the power) of God; he didn't have the authority to use the name of Jesus Christ. Sometimes you hear people say that Jesus Christ came to restore what Adam lost in the garden of Eden. This assertion is not accurate; it's untrue. What the Lord Jesus did for mankind is unprecedented. It has never been seen nor heard. The Lord didn't restore mankind back to Adam; rather, He gave mankind something that's entirely different, brand-new, and never existed in the history of creation. The one who is in Christ, the Christian, which forms the body of Christ or the church, is born of God. That man never existed before. He's a new creature, according to 2 Corinthians 5:17 (KJV). The Christian is the greatest and most glorious creation of God. He excels in glory and power. He's born of God; he's a son of God; and he's a god (John 1:13; John 10:34; Psalm 82:6). If what Adam lost to Satan in the garden of Eden were a car, what the Lord Jesus Christ came to give back to mankind would be an airplane. So it's not "like for like." The life from the Lord Jesus Christ is far more superior to the one lost by Adam. If the Adamic garment were a car, the best robe that has come through Christ is an airplane. A car and an airplane are not in the same class; they're not in any way similar. One is driven on the road, but the other flies in the air at high altitude, beyond physical obstacles and limitations. No wonder Ephesians 2:6 says, "And God raised us up with Christ and seated us with him in the heavenly realms in Christ Jesus." Since the believer has been raised and seated with Christ, the question then is, Where is Christ sitting right now, together with the believer? The answer is found in the word of God, which speaks about "his incomparably great power for us who believe. That power is the same as the mighty strength he exerted when he raised Christ from the dead and seated him at his right hand in the heavenly realms, *far above all rule and authority, power and dominion, and every name that is invoked*, not only in the present age but also in the one to come" (Ephesians 1:19–21). Therefore, those that are in Christ, the children of God, have superior power and authority over Satan and his demons. Satan and his demons have been stripped of their stolen Adamic garment. The Lord Jesus Christ was manifested that He might destroy the works of the devil (1 John 3:8). Colossians 2:15 further says, "And having disarmed the powers and authorities, he made a public spectacle of them, triumphing over them by the cross." The devil has been disarmed and stripped of the Adamic authority that he stole from Adam. He has been stripped of his stolen power, defeated, and disarmed. The Lord Jesus Christ made a public show of their disgraceful defeat, triumphing over them by the cross. So don't ever get intimidated by Satan or his demons; you're far more superior to them. If you ever come across their nefarious activities around you, just cast them out in the name of the Lord Jesus Christ. You have received the best robe and the ring of dominion. One way of exercising this Christ-given dominion is in casting out demons and putting a stop to the illegal operation of the devil in the lives of men (Luke 10:17–19; Mark 16:17). It is the heritage and honor of God's children, the saints, to enforce and execute the victory of Christ over Satan and his demons on the cross. This is why the psalmist, by the Holy Spirit, wrote concerning the saints, anyone that's in Christ, saying, "To bind their kings with chains, and their nobles with fetters of iron; to execute on them the written judgment—This honor have all His saints. Praise the Lord" (Psalm 149:8–9 NKJV). In the NIV, verse 9 is rendered as "to carry out the sentence written against them—this is the glory of all his faithful people." The word *glory* is used instead of *honor* in the NIV. God's faithful people are to carry out the sentence written against the devil and his agents. Child of God, it is both your honor and glory to cast out demons and enforce the judgment that the Lord Jesus Christ has written against the devil and his agents. The Son of God was manifested that He might destroy the works of the devil. It is our honor and glory to enforce the destruction of the works of the devil in the lives of men through the power of the Holy Ghost and in the mighty name of our Lord Jesus Christ. This is our heritage in Christ. Hallelujah!

## Summary

The Parable of the Good Samaritan has been unveiled in this chapter. The underlying story reveals one of the most incredible hidden messages of the Lord Jesus Christ regarding the divine plan of God for the salvation of all mankind. This parable reveals the genesis of the problems of mankind and the salvation plan of God for all mankind through His Son, Jesus Christ. From the underlying message, the certain man is seen to symbolize Adam, who stands in the place of all mankind. As Adam journeyed through life from the garden of Eden, he was severely attacked by Satan and his demonic agents, using sin as the weapon of attack. During the attack, the first thing they did to Adam was to strip him of his garment. Since his garment was the first thing that was stolen from him, this shows that the garment of Adam was the main thing that made the devil to attack him. This garment symbolized the power, authority, glory, and dominion, which God gave to Adam when he was created. Following the stealing of his garment, the devil and his agents wounded mankind and left him half dead. By this, man, which is both a spiritual and physical being, died spiritually and was only physically alive. He became separated eternally from God, his Maker. While Adam was lying helpless in the way, the law of Moses accidentally came his way but couldn't help him. The reason being that the law of Moses was weak, powerless, and useless and didn't have the capacity to help this badly wounded man. Similarly, the prophets came by chance along the way of Adam, coming very close to helping him but could not. Although both the law and the prophets couldn't help the wounded Adam, however, the prophets came closer to helping him than the law. While the law was very far away from helping the wounded man, the prophets, however, came very close to offering him help. The prophets approached him to have a closer look, signifying how the prophets, over the years and generations, brought mankind closer to God. The most notable among these prophets is John the Baptist, who came in the spirit and power of Elijah. He was the one who identified Jesus as the Christ and Lamb of God that takes away the sin of the whole world. John the Baptist was also the one that announced the Lord Jesus and prepared the way for Him. He was the one that baptized the Lord in the River Jordan, letting the people know that the Lord Jesus Christ was greater than him and that the Lord Jesus is the one that baptizes with the Holy Ghost and with fire. In spite of all the great things that were done by the prophets, however, they couldn't save the severely wounded mankind. The Good Samaritan then showed up along the line, who symbolizes the Lord Jesus Christ Himself. While the law and the prophets came by chance to the road where the wounded mankind laid, Christ came to that same road, having carefully planned His journey along that road, knowing that mankind was in danger of falling among those thieves and be seriously attacked. It is interesting to note that before the Lord Jesus Christ went to the cross to save mankind, Moses and Elijah, representing the law and the prophets, appeared and spoke with Him on the mount of transfiguration. The law and the prophets preceded the coming of Christ. Through Christ's vicarious death on the cross of Calvary, the wounded mankind was treated and resuscitated. The Lord's broken body brought healing and wholeness to mankind. His blood, symbolized in the parable by wine, was poured on the wounds of mankind for the remission of his sins. That same blood gave eternal life to mankind. The life of the flesh is in the blood; it's the blood that makes atonement for one's life (Leviticus 17:11). As a result of the work that Christ did on the cross, the fullness of the Holy Spirit is now made available to all mankind, symbolized as the pouring of oil on the wounds of the man in the parable. All these happened on the cross of Calvary when the Lord Jesus Christ paid the ultimate price for the salvation and redemption of all mankind. The Lord Jesus didn't die for a selected group of people. He died once and for all for the salvation of all mankind. He completed the work of salvation for mankind and said, "It is finished" (John 19:30). All done and sorted, nothing else left to be done for the salvation of mankind. He paid the price in full. All that is required of any man to appropriate this great salvation is to repent and receive the Lord Jesus Christ, believing in his heart that Jesus Christ is the Son of God and that God raised Him from the dead and confessing with his mouth that Jesus Christ is his Lord and Savior. This is all that's required to receive and appropriate this great salvation that has been made available to all mankind. While hanging lifeless on the cross, a Roman soldier pierced His side with a spear, causing blood and water to gush out from his body, which is symbolized in the parable as the pouring of oil and wine on the wounds of mankind. The Lord Jesus bore the pains and grief of the wounded mankind in His own body, symbolized in the parable by his own donkey. He carried mankind to an inn, symbolizing the birth of the church, a people that are being treated and revived by the living word of God. The church is both a people and a place—a people redeemed by grace and a place where the rescued mankind is being revived and continuously fed by the living word of God, which is medicine and health for the human life, according to Proverbs 4:22. The Holy Spirit is the chief overseer of the church of Christ here on earth. He's symbolized by the innkeeper, the One taking care of the rescued mankind in the inn. The Lord Jesus has made a down payment of two thousand years, indicating the church dispensation, a period during which the rescued mankind should be revived and cared for in the inn; although there's the possibility of this extending beyond two thousand years if the Holy Spirit, symbolized by the innkeeper, requires more time to fully revive and restore mankind in accordance with God's divine will and purpose. On making the down payment of two thousand years, the Lord Jesus Christ left the earth and was received up in heaven, to return later when the time is due. Since then, the Holy Spirit has been the One on earth nourishing, treating, and taking care of the rescued mankind. This is why the Bible says, "It is the Spirit Who gives life [He is the Life-giver]; the flesh conveys no benefit whatever [there is no profit in it]. The words (truths) that I have been speaking to you are spirit and life" (John 6:63 AMPC). The Holy Spirit is the One that's giving life to the rescued mankind, reviving him to full state of health, vitality, wholeness, and perfection. This is why God's word assures us that "if the Spirit of Him Who raised up Jesus from the dead dwells in you, [then] He Who raised up Christ Jesus from the dead will also restore to life your mortal (short-lived, perishable) bodies through His Spirit Who dwells in you" (Romans 8:11 AMPC). As a result of the work of the Holy Spirit who dwells in us, we are being revived and restored to full vitality by the Spirit that dwells in us. Following the down payment of two thousand years for the revival of the rescued mankind, the Lord promised that He would return afterward. If two thousand years are added to the year that the church was born, which is the year that the Lord Jesus resurrected and is the same as the year that the Holy Spirit came down to earth on Pentecost Day, then one would find that the time before the Lord Jesus returns is extremely short. In fact, the number of years remaining for the church to clock two thousand years old is in single digits. This is how close the time is. Our Lord is returning soon. How prepared are you to meet your Lord and Savior? Are you ready? This brings us nicely to the next chapter, where we see ten virgins, five wise and prepared, while the other five were foolish and unprepared for the return of the Lord. Let's learn from the five wise virgins and make ourselves ready for the Lord's soon return.

# CHAPTER 5

## The Parable of the Ten Virgins (Matthew 25:1–13)

Then the kingdom of heaven shall be likened to ten virgins who took their lamps and went out to meet the bridegroom. Now five of them were wise, and five were foolish. Those who were foolish took their lamps and took no oil with them, but the wise took oil in their vessels with their lamps. But while the bridegroom was delayed, they all slumbered and slept. And at midnight a cry was heard: "Behold, the bridegroom is coming; go out to meet him!" Then all those virgins arose and trimmed their lamps. And the foolish said to the wise, "Give us some of your oil, for our lamps are going out." But the wise answered, saying, "No, lest there should not be enough for us and you; but go rather to those who sell, and buy for yourselves." And while they went to buy, the bridegroom came, and those who were ready went in with him to the wedding; and the door was shut. Afterward the other virgins came also, saying, "Lord, Lord, open to us!" But he answered and said, "Assuredly, I say to you, I do not know you." Watch therefore, for you know neither the day nor the hour in which the Son of Man is coming.

—Matthew 25:1–13 NKJV

The Parable of the Ten Virgins is very powerful. It's about the only parable in the Bible that's exclusively for the church of Christ. Most parables of the Lord Jesus pertained mostly to the Jews, Gentiles, the world, and entire mankind. However, the Parable of the Ten Virgins is about the only parable told by the Lord Jesus which pertains exclusively to the church of Christ.

## Unveiling the Parable of the Ten Virgins

Let us begin to unveil the Parable of the Ten Virgins in chronological order for full understanding of the underlying message.

1. *The ten virgins*: "The kingdom of heaven shall be likened to *ten virgins*" (vs 1). To unveil the ten virgins, let's begin by first defining the key word *virgin*. *Who is a virgin?* We know so many definitions of what a virgin is, but let's consider those definitions that are not so obvious but still accurately define a virgin. A virgin can be defined as someone who's untouched, unspoiled, untainted, untarnished, pristine, unadulterated, pure, flawless, immaculate, spotless, unblemished, stainless, unpolluted, undefiled, intact, unaffected, preserved, unused, perfect, etc. The people that are like this can only be found in Christ, according to God's word, which says, "If anyone belongs to Christ, then he is *made new*. The old things have gone; *everything is made new*!" (2 Corinthians 5:17 ICB). This is the classic scriptural definition of a virgin. The one who is in Christ is made new, meaning he is unused, untouched, spotless, intact, pure, unadulterated, stainless, flawless, etc., all of which are accurate definitions of a virgin. The one who is in Christ is a brand-new person. He's never been seen before. In fact, the Christian has never been seen before. He never existed before now. The Christian is unprecedented. There is no precedence for the one who belongs to Christ. He's a never-seen-before type of creation. That is the meaning of "if any man be in Christ, he is a new creation" (2 Corinthians 5:17 NKJV). The one who belongs to Christ is a new creation of God. He's unspotted and unpolluted, keeping

himself "from being polluted by the world" (James 1:27). So we have seen that the one who belongs to Christ is made brand-new, made a virgin. We also see the apostle Paul refer directly to the Christian as being a virgin in 2 Corinthians 11:2, when he said, "I am jealous for you with a godly jealousy. I promised you to one husband, to Christ, so that I might present you as a *pure virgin* to him." The Christian is a pure virgin to God. The new man in Christ is unprecedented. There has never been a Christian before in the world. When God made Adam, he (Adam) wasn't a Christian. He was made in the image and likeness of God and same with all of mankind, but the new man in Christ (Christian) is not only made by God but born of God. Adam, the first man, was made in the image and likeness of God, but the Christian is born of God. They are completely two different things: to be made in the image and to be born. They are not the same. The Christians are those "who were born, not of blood, nor of the will of the flesh, nor of the will of man, but of God" (John 1:13). Adam was made in the image and likeness of God. Every man and woman, before coming to Christ, was made in the image and likeness of God, but when they become born again, they are now born of God. These are two different things. So there are two types of men on earth, those made in the image and likeness of God, and all men are like that, and those born of God. These are those that have received Jesus as their Lord and Savior. They are the ones that have eternal life. These are the ones the Lord Jesus said to Nicodemus in John 3:3, 5 that "what is born of Spirit is spirit, and what is born of flesh is flesh. Except a man is born of water and the Spirit, he cannot enter the kingdom of God." The water is the word of God (Ephesians 5:26), and the Spirit is the Holy Ghost. The word of God is God; the spirit of God is God. That's what it means to be born of God. First Peter 1:23 makes us know that we are born again by the incorruptible word of the living God. So every Christian is born of the word of God and the spirit of God, and we will later see the power of the Word and Spirit in this parable as we begin to unveil the different elements of the parable. Therefore, all ten virgins are ten born-again believers. This is not like five Jews and five Gentiles or five believers and five nonbelievers; no, all ten virgins are ten believers. It makes this very interesting as this is about the only parable of our Lord Jesus Christ that is exclusively related to the church of Christ. Every believer is a virgin before God—untainted, undefiled, unspotted from this world. Christianity did not come from Christ's death on the cross but from the resurrection of Christ. Christianity came from the resurrection of Christ. The sin of Adam was addressed on the cross. The Lord Jesus was the first Christian. When He was raised back to life, He was born anew; that's why the Scripture says, "You are my Son, today I have begotten you" (Hebrews 5:5; Acts 13:33; Psalm 2:7). All of mankind died in Christ on the cross, but not all of mankind resurrected with Him. It's only those who have received Christ as the Lord and Savior of their lives, people now referred to as Christians, that are the ones that resurrected with Him, only those that have taken that step of faith and confessed Jesus Christ as their Lord and Savior and believe in Him, according to Romans 10:10. Every child of God is a virgin, brand-new before God. The ten virgins are perfect, flawless, untainted, spotless. What then makes the foolish and the wise virgins? The answer to this pertinent question will become more obvious while unveiling this parable. It has already been established that the ten virgins are ten believers, each having a lamp. What does the lamp symbolize?

2. *The lamp*: "…who took their *lamps* and went out to meet the bridegroom" (vs 1). The lamp symbolizes the word of God. In Psalm 119:105 (NKJV), the Scripture says, "Your *Word is a lamp* to my feet and a light to my path." Spiritually, the lamp is a prophetic symbol for the word of God. It represents the word of God. A lamp produces light for illumination. This is the reason why the word of God illuminates; it gives light, according to Psalm 119:130 (NKJV), which says, "The entrance of Your words gives light; It gives understanding to the simple." This same Word, from the beginning, has been with God. In Him was life, and the life was the light of all mankind (John 1:1, 4).

This is why Psalm 18:28 further says, "You, Lord, keep my lamp burning; my God turns my darkness into light." Since all ten virgins had individual lamps, it means they all had the word of God. All ten virgins had the word of God. First, all ten virgins were born again, so they have been born of the word of God, according to 1 Peter 1:23. All ten virgins heard the same word of God, as expressed in Hebrews 4:2.

> The same gospel that was preached to us was also preached to them, but the Word preached did not profit them not being mixed with faith in them that heard it.

The lamp symbolizes the word of God. Since all ten virgins individually had a lamp, it means all ten virgins individually had the word of God.

3. *The oil*: "Those who were foolish took their lamps and took no *oil* with them, but the wise took *oil* in their vessels with their lamps" (vs 3–4). The oil is a prophetic symbol for the anointing of the Holy Spirit of God. That is why Psalm 23:5 says, "You anoint my head with oil; my cup overflows." Similarly, Isaiah 61:1 and Luke 4:18 say, "The Spirit of the Lord God is upon me because He's anointed me." The AMPC version of Zechariah 4:6 gives us a clearer description, saying, "Not by might, nor by power, but by My Spirit [of Whom the oil is a symbol], says the Lord of hosts" (Zechariah 4:6 AMPC). In Acts 10:38, we learn "how God anointed Jesus of Nazareth with the Holy Ghost and with power, who went about doing good and healing all that were oppressed of the devil for God was with Him." The Lord Jesus was anointed with the Holy Ghost. The oil symbolizes the anointing, the Holy Spirit.

4. *The wise and the foolish virgins*: "Now five of them were foolish, five of them were wise. Those who were *foolish* took their lamps and *took no oil with them*, but the *wise took oil in their vessels* with their lamps" (vs 2–4). Here we are given the reason why five of

the virgins were wise and five foolish. In verses 3 and 4, we have the vital information about what made the difference between the wise and the foolish virgins: The wise took oil in the vessels of their lamp, but the foolish did not. Just that little thing that the five wise virgins did made the difference between them and the five foolish virgins. The difference between the wise and foolish virgins was the foresight, knowledge, and insight they had. The wise were proactive; they carefully reasoned and anticipated that it was possible for the bridegroom to delay. However, the foolish virgins assumed that everything was hunky-dory. They never bothered to think about the possibility that the bridegroom could delay, and nighttime would come, and they would need to trim their lamps. The difference is the revelation the wise virgins had: the knowledge and foresight. The wise virgins sat and thought there may be delay, what would happen if the bridegroom were delayed? They decided to take extra oil with them. The foolish virgins didn't think of that possibility. They didn't have insight and foresight. (We will see later that it was the Holy Spirit that inspired the wise virgins to take extra oil because they walked in the Spirit; whereas the foolish virgins were carnal and not spiritual, so they walked in spiritual darkness.) The foolish virgins had the lamp, which symbolizes the word of God, but they didn't have the oil, which symbolizes the Spirit of God. How often do we see this today in the body of Christ, believers rich in theology but with no anointing of the Holy Spirit? The wise virgins had the word of God and were also full of the Holy Ghost. This is the only way it works. Every believer needs both the Word and the Spirit of God. This is God's expectation of His children. Our Father wants His children to abide in His word and Holy Spirit. The Word without the Spirit is the classic definition of religion, which, according to 2 Corinthians 3:6, is the letter that kills.

> Who also made us sufficient as ministers of the new covenant, not of the letter but of the Spirit; for the letter kills, but the Spirit gives life. (2 Corinthians 3:6 NKJV)

Letter is the word of God without the Spirit. That's theological religion. The lamp alone is religion. The Word of God without the Spirit of God is religion. The Lord Jesus said, "It is the Spirit who gives life; the flesh profits nothing. The words that I speak to you are spirit, and they are life" (John 6:63 NKJV). The Word of God is both Spirit and life. It is the Spirit that gives life to the Word. The Holy Spirit is the mystery behind the word of God. He is the power behind the word of God. Without the Holy Spirit, the word of God is not different from any other ordinary word. If you have the word of God, and the Holy Ghost is not there, it is nothing. The word that works is that which goes together with the Spirit. The Word that brings transformation to the life of a man or woman is the Word that's full of the Spirit of God. It is the Spirit that does the work of transformation. The Spirit of God is the secret behind the word of God. This was demonstrated in Genesis 1:1–3, where the Holy Spirit moved upon the surface of the waters, doing the groundwork, before God spoke the words of creation to being.

> In the beginning God created the heaven and the earth. And the earth was without form, and void; and darkness was upon the face of the deep. *And the Spirit of God moved upon the face of the waters*. And God said, Let there be light: and there was light. (Genesis 1:1–3 KJV)

Before God released the word, the Holy Spirit was in the background, doing the groundwork. The Holy Ghost is the One behind the scenes of everything that the word of God does.

5. *The carnal (foolish) virgins versus the spiritual (wise) virgins*: The foolish virgins were carnal and not spiritual, so they walked in spiritual darkness. The scripture in Ephesians, chapter 5, gives us more insights into what it means to be spiritually wise or foolish. It says, "So be careful how you live. Don't live like fools, but like those who are wise. Make the most of every opportunity in these evil days. Don't act thoughtlessly, but understand what the Lord

wants you to do. Don't be drunk with wine, because that will ruin your life. Instead, be filled with the Holy Spirit" (Ephesians 5:15–18 NLT). This scripture can easily be juxtaposed with the Parable of the Ten Virgins. Both passages have very similar messages. From this we know that the foolish virgins were not careful how they lived; they lived recklessly. They lived like fools, not making the most of every opportunity that came their way. They were thoughtless and couldn't fathom the will of God or what the Lord wanted them to do because of their carnality. They didn't have the spiritual insight and understanding to know that the Lord wanted them to take extra oil with them to the wedding. The foolish virgins were drunk with wine and not filled with the Holy Spirit, which ruined their lives. This is so sad!

On the contrary, the wise virgins ticked all the right boxes. They were extremely careful of how they lived. They lived wisely, making the most of every opportunity that came their way. They were thoughtful, always meditating on the Scriptures and understanding the will of God. They knew what the Lord wanted them to do as they had spiritual insight and foresight. They had the spiritual insight and understanding to know that the Lord wanted them to take extra oil with them to the wedding. The wise virgins were sober and not drunk with wine. They were filled with the Holy Spirit, which empowered them to preserve their own lives. The foolish virgins were not people of the Spirit; they were carnally minded. No wonder Scriptures admonish us.

> For to be carnally minded is death; but to be spiritually minded is life and peace. Because the carnal mind is enmity against God: for it is not subject to the law of God, neither indeed can be. So then they that are in the flesh cannot please God. (Romans 8:6–8 KJV)

We must be men and women that are spiritually minded. We must not give room to carnality and coldness of the Spirit. The wise virgins were men and women of God that had the Spirit and were thus led by the Holy Spirit.

> For as many as are led by the Spirit of God,
> they are the sons of God. (Romans 8:14 KJV)

To be led by the spirit of God is the hallmark of sonship in the kingdom of our God. It's the hallmark of spiritual maturity. The Passion Translation (TPT) rendering of this passage is particularly illuminating. It says, "The mature children of God are *those* who are moved by the impulses of the Holy Spirit" (Romans 8:14 TPT). The italicized word *those* is highlighted in the footnote as being emphasized in the Greek text as "those and only those." This therefore means that "those and only those" that are moved by the impulses of the Holy Spirit are the mature children of God. So to be considered a matured child of God, one must be moved by the impulses of the Holy Spirit, not by the impulses of the flesh or emotions. That's so profound! The Holy Spirit is our authenticator. The Spirit Himself bears witness with our spirit that we are the children of God (Romans 8:16). The believer is sealed by the Holy Spirit. The Holy Spirit is the believer's authenticator and authentication. He's the validator of the believer. This is why 1 John 5:6–7 (KJV) states that in heaven, the Father, the Word, and the Spirit bear record, and they are one (vs 6). Meanwhile in earth, the Spirit, the water, and the blood bear witness, and they agree as one (vs 7). The Spirit bears record in heaven and bears witness on earth. When you become born-again, the Spirit bears witness of your salvation and sonship in the earth and records this in heaven. His witness of you must agree with the witnesses of the water (the word of God) and the blood (the life of Christ you received at salvation). The witness from all three must agree as one. That means you must have been saved and have the life of Christ, obedient and abiding in the word of God, and full of the Holy Spirit and walking in the Spirit. The believer must have an existing and subsisting relationship with the Holy Spirit. Because the wise virgins were led by the Spirit, they were spiritually inspired to take extra oil with them. The Spirit is light, and when you walk closely with

Him, you're always in the light. When you walk in the light, you will never walk in darkness. The foolish virgins had no light in them, so they walked perpetually in darkness. This reminds us of the words of Asaph in Psalm 82:5–7 (KJV):

> They know not, neither will they understand; they walk on in darkness: all the foundations of the earth are out of course. I have said, Ye are gods; and all of you are children of the most High. But ye shall die like men and fall like one of the princes.

The foolish virgins walked in darkness, unlike the wise virgins who walked in the light of the Spirit. That is why Proverbs 4:18 says, "The path of the righteous is like the morning sun, shining ever brighter till the full light of day."

6. *The insightful conversation between the foolish and wise virgins*: Let's consider this interesting conversation between the foolish and wise virgins in verse 8. I'm particularly captivated by the insightful response given by the wise virgins in verses 9 and 10:

> And the foolish said unto the wise, Give us of your oil; for our lamps are gone out. But the wise answered, saying, Not so; lest there be not enough for us and you: *but go ye rather to them that sell, and buy for yourselves.* And while they went to buy, the bridegroom came; and they that were ready went in with him to the marriage: and the door was shut. (Matthew 25:9–10 KJV)

The italicized portion of verse 9 indicates that there are people that sell this oil. That means there's a place the oil can be bought, and there's a currency that can be used for that transaction. The three curious questions here are, Who are those people that sell this oil? How do you buy this oil from them that sell? Do you require silver, gold, or money to buy the oil from them that sell? These three questions are carefully answered in the next item below.

7. *Go to them that sell this oil, and buy for yourself:* In verse 9, the wise virgins said to the foolish virgins, "Go to them that sell," meaning there are people that sell this oil. You need to buy. To buy this oil, the Holy Spirit of God, you don't need dollars or pound sterling. In Acts 8:18–23, Simon the Sorcerer thought he could buy this oil with money, but Peter responded by saying, "May your money perish with you, because you thought you could buy the gift of God with money!" (Acts 8:20). You don't need silver or gold. The currency needed to buy this oil is found in Isaiah 55:1–3; it's called thirst. You can have all the silver and gold on earth, but if you don't have a hunger and thirst for the Holy Spirit, you can't have Him. Our Lord, speaking in the beatitude in Matthew 5:6, said, "Blessed are they that do hunger and thirst for righteousness for they shall be filled." You need a hunger; you need a thirst. Every human being has a thirst. You must thirst for the continuous infilling of the Holy Spirit. The price for buying this oil is a thirst. In John 7:37–38 (KJV), our Lord Jesus declared on the last day of the feast, "If any man thirst, let him come to me and drink, as the Scriptures have said, he that believes in me out of His belly shall flow rivers of living water." The Lord Jesus is coming back soon. Earlier, in chapter 4, we found that the dispensation of the church is for two thousand years. Hosea 6:2 states, "After two days He will revive us…" In 2 Peter 3:8, one day is like a thousand years and a thousand years like one day. The two days is a prophetic symbol for two thousand years. The wedding the ten virgins went for is the marriage supper of the Lamb, recorded in Revelation 19:9–11. The Lord Jesus is coming back soon. The devil will keep many believers in church, busy with so many carnal and worldly activities. You can be very busy for God and yet be completely out of touch with God. The five foolish virgins were very busy. They may have gone to get cakes and gifts as presents for the bridegroom. God wants us to hunger more for Him. He wants us to hunger for

His word and Spirit. Let's hunger for God. In Ezekiel 47:1–5, we see the different levels that are attainable in the river of the Holy Spirit. Water is a prophetic symbol for the Holy Spirit, as earlier seen in the Words of our Lord Jesus Christ in John 7:38. There's a level of infilling of the Holy Ghost that's to the ankle, a level that's to the knees, a level that's to the waist, and a level that's fully submerged, where a believer is completely submerged and swimming in the anointing of the Holy Spirit. This last level is God's plan for His people, the level where the water becomes a river that requires the individual to be fully submerged and swim in the water. This is God's desire for His children, and it's the same level that the Lord Jesus was referring to in John 7:37–38, saying, "Rivers of living water will flow from within them." It takes genuine hunger and thirst to move from level to level in the depth of the Holy Spirit. Our Father wants His children to swim in His Spirit. He wants us to swim in the river of the Holy Ghost. Our Father wants us to be full and replete with His precious Holy Spirit. Like it was with our Lord Jesus Christ, in John 3:34, we too have received the fullness of the Spirit. The Father gives the Holy Spirit to us without measure. This is why the Word says, "And to know this love that surpasses knowledge—that you may be filled to the measure of all the fullness of God" (Ephesians 3:19). In John 1:16, we further learn that "out of his fullness we have all received grace in place of grace already given." God has made the fullness of the Spirit available to any man that's in Christ. You only need to thirst, hunger, and ask, and you will receive (Matthew 7:7).

## The believer-Christian dichotomy

The Parable of the Ten Virgins underscores the believer-Christian dichotomy. While the believer is anyone who believes in Jesus Christ as Lord and Savior, however, the Christian is any believer in whom Christ has been formed. It is therefore possible to be a believer and not be a Christian; whereas, all Christians are believers. The Holy Spirit is the difference between the believer and the Christian. There are believers without the Holy Spirit, these cannot be referred to as Christians as these do not have the spirit of Christ. The Scripture says, "If anyone does not have the Spirit of Christ, they do not belong to Christ" (Romans 8:9). Therefore, what authenticates a man as belonging to Christ is the Holy Spirit. It doesn't matter the depth of theology or knowledge of God's word; if a man doesn't have the Holy Spirit, he's a mere believer of Christ and not a Christian. The foolish and wise virgins are a contrast that reflect the believer-Christian dichotomy. The foolish virgins were very sound in theology, having the lamp of God's word but were far from knowing and walking by the spirit of God; they were mere believers.

On the other hand, the wise virgins were sound in both theology and in their walk with the Holy Spirit. They belonged to Christ and lived like Him; they were Christians. Every Christian is a believer, but not every believer is a Christian. Every man receives Christ as a believer and then matures into a Christian. If a man refuses to grow or mature from a believer to a Christian, he will remain as a mere believer, not looking anything like Christ. The perfect will of God is for every believer to grow and mature into a Christian. The Holy Spirit is the One that transforms a believer to a Christian. The Holy Spirit is the difference between a believer and a Christian. The Holy Spirit is the seal of Christianity (Ephesians 1:13). Being led by the Holy Spirit is the hallmark of sonship in the kingdom of God (Romans 8:14). Walking with the Holy Spirit is the whole essence of Christianity. God's idea for mankind was for Him to put the Holy Spirit inside man. All man needed was the Holy Ghost. One of my most favorite quotes of all time was given by William Temple, who was the ninety-eighth archbishop of Canterbury. The quote goes thus, "It's no good to show me a book like king Lear or Hamlet and ask me to write a book like that; Shakespeare could do that, but I can't. And it's no good to show me a life like Jesus Christ and ask me to live a life like that; Jesus could do that, but I can't. However, if the genius of Shakespeare would come and live in me, then I would write books like Shakespeare's; and if the Spirit that was in Jesus would come and live in me, then I would live a life like that of Jesus Christ." This is so profound. If these golden words from William Temple were directly written in the Bible, we would have been using that scriptural passage as the classic textbook definition of Christianity. Simply put, Christianity is man having the indwelling spirit of Christ so that he can live like Jesus Christ. The spirit of Christ in you is what makes you a Christian. It's possible to be a believer and yet not a Christian. You can hold a position of leadership in your local church or in the body of Christ, and you're not a Christian. Church attendance alone does not make a Christian. The spirit of Jesus Christ indwelling and active in a man's life, causing him to manifest the fruit of the Spirit, is what makes him a Christian. The *Christ* in *Christian* means Jesus Christ, while the *-ian* means like. Therefore, Christian means to be Christlike. So a Christian is someone who's like Jesus Christ, and this is because that person has the spirit of Jesus Christ. This is why it's incorrect to say there are Christian thieves, Christian prostitutes, Christian liars, Christian scammers, etc. This is a fallacy of contradictions. If we say somebody is a Christian and a thief at the same time, the implication is that, since the person is like Christ, it means Christ is a thief. But if we say no, Christ is never a thief, therefore it means this person was never like Christ. The body of Christ must recognize and be able to differentiate between a believer and a Christian (someone who's like Christ). Every man comes to Christ as a believer and then matures into a Christian.

In Acts 19:1–7 (KJV), the apostle Paul came across twelve believers (disciples) in Ephesus and asked them if they had received the Holy Ghost since they believed. They gave a very surprising response: "He said unto them, Have ye received the Holy Ghost since ye believed? And they said unto him, We have not so much as heard whether there be any Holy Ghost. And he said unto them, Unto what then were ye baptized? And they said, Unto John's baptism" (Acts 19:2–3). At that point, these twelve followers of Christ were just believers. They hadn't heard about the Holy Ghost at all, let alone received Him. The apostle Paul proceeded to lay his hands on them and prayed for them in the name of the Lord Jesus Christ: "And when Paul had laid his hands upon them, the Holy Ghost came on them; and they spake with tongues and prophesied. And all the men were about twelve." At this point, these believers had now become Christians. It's the Holy Spirit that transforms a believer into a Christian. Until and unless a believer is filled with the Holy Ghost and lives daily by His inner leading, it's not possible for that believer to live like Christ. It is the Holy Spirit that gives life and ability to the Christian. That is the reason why the Lord Jesus said, "It is the Spirit who gives life; the flesh profits nothing. The words that I speak to you are spirit, and they are life" (John 6:63 NKJV). It is the Holy Spirit that gives divine life and causes Christ to be formed in the life of the believer. The apostle Paul, writing to the church in Galatia, let them know that they were his little children, and he was laboring for them in intense prayers and ministry of the Word, until Christ was formed in them.

> My little children, for whom I labor in birth again until Christ is formed in you. (Galatians 4:19 NKJV)

Every believer must arrive at that destination, where Christ is formed in them. That can only happen by the ministry of the Holy Spirit and the word of God. The time has come when the true worshippers must worship the Father in Spirit and in truth, for this is the only way God desires to be worshipped, according to His word in John 4:23–24.

## The bridegroom was delayed

"But while the bridegroom was delayed, they all slumbered and slept" (vs 5). In the Parable of the Wedding Feast in chapter 3, the bridegroom was scripturally identified as our Lord Jesus Christ Himself. In this parable, we are informed that the bridegroom was delayed. This means the possibility is there for the Lord's return to be delayed. We see the same situation in the Parable of the Good Samaritan earlier in chapter 4, when the Good Samaritan (symbolizing the Lord Jesus) told the innkeeper (symbolizing the Holy Spirit) that if He spends anything additional, He would pay it back when He returns. This shows that the possibility is there for the dispensation of the church to exceed two thousand years. There's a precedence for this occurrence in the Old Testament. God told Abraham that his descendants would go down to Egypt and become slaves. He said He would visit them after four hundred years (Genesis 15:13–14). Meanwhile, the children of Israel ended up spending four hundred and thirty years in Egypt (Exodus 12:40), even though the prophetic word stated four hundred years. Therefore, we must not despair if peradventure the Lord tarries. We must continue to serve the Lord, win souls for His kingdom, and do good to those around us, irrespective of whether the Lord returns at the stated prophetic time, or He tarries.

It is extremely important that we take note of the italicized portion in the following phrase: "but while the bridegroom *was delayed.*" The italicized portion implies that the bridegroom did not cause the delay Himself, rather He was delayed by another. So can someone else cause the Lord Jesus to delay His return? According to the Bible, the answer is a resounding yes. Scripturally, the two people that can cause the return of the Lord Jesus Christ to be delayed are God the Father and the church. When the Lord Jesus, following His glorious resurrection, was asked by His disciples when the kingdom would be restored to Israel, "He said to them: 'It is not for you to know the times or dates the Father has set by his own authority'" (Acts 1:7). By this response, He implied that the Father is the One who calls the shot on when He returns to earth for His millennial reign. So it is possible for the Father to shorten or extend the time as He pleases, in line with His ultimate divine will and purpose for mankind. This is further supported by the words of the Lord Jesus Christ in the Gospels, saying, "But about that day or hour no one knows, not even the angels in heaven, *nor the Son,* but only the Father" (Mark 13:32; Matthew 24:36). So we have seen that it is God the Father who will determine the day and hour of the Lord's return.

The second person that can delay the Lord's return is the church of Christ. According to the words of the Lord Jesus, "This gospel of the kingdom will be preached in the whole world as a testimony to all nations, and then the end will come" (Matthew 24:14). Without ambiguity, the Lord Jesus has made it clear that this gospel will be preached in the whole world as a testimony to all nations, and then He would return to earth for His millennial reign. This therefore puts the responsibility on the church of Christ to ensure that the mandate for the Great Commission given to the church is speedily completed. The church must engage tirelessly in evangelistic work of ministry, ensuring that the whole world gets the opportunity to receive this precious message of salvation for all mankind, and then the end would come. Isn't the Lord gracious? He doesn't want anyone to miss out from being given the opportunity to hear the good news of the gospel. For this reason, His return can be delayed if that would allow more souls to be harvested into the kingdom of the Father. These are the two reasons that can possibly cause the return of the Lord to be delayed. Believers must continue therefore to tirelessly witness for the Lord and bring harvest of souls into our Father's kingdom. This is a major way of ensuring that the Lord's return is not delayed. As was discussed earlier in chapter 2, we have been well kitted for the Great Commission with shoes on our feet. We must arise therefore and make the best use of our glorious shoes, for "how beautiful are the feet of those who preach the gospel of peace, who bring glad tidings of good things!" (Romans 10:15 NKJV).

## The mystery of the wedding bride

It is worth noting that in this Parable of the Ten Virgins and all other parables given by our Lord Jesus involving a bridegroom and wedding settings, there's usually nothing said about the bride. We only hear of the bridegroom and the invited guests. For example, in this parable, there was a bridegroom and ten virgins who were invited as guests to the wedding. There's nothing said about the bride. The reason is because there's no separate bride; a collection of people from the invited guests makes up the bride. In this parable, all ten virgins were the wedding guests, but the five wise virgins that made it to the wedding feast now become the bride. Please note that it's a bride, singular. A collection of the chosen guests makes the bride. In Matthew 24:14, we understand that "many are called, but few are chosen." The many called are the wedding guests, while the chosen few collectively become the bride. The implication of this for the church today is that not everyone that goes to church is a bride of Christ. Everyone in church is a guest, but only those that have kept themselves undefiled, pure, and without wrinkle (Ephesians 5:27) are the chosen bride. Everyone that comes to Christ is a believer; however, it's only those that live daily in total obedience to His word and are yielded to the leading of His Holy Spirit that are the bride of Christ. The bride of Christ is holy, spotless, and absolutely loyal to Him. The word of God is the most supreme authority in the life of a bride.

In every nation, there are citizens, but not every citizen is patriotic. Patriotic citizens are loyal to their nation. They are responsible and law-abiding citizens. In the same vein, in the kingdom of Christ, everyone that believes in Him is a believer; however, it's only those believers that are loyal to the lordship of Christ and are fully yielded to His word and Holy Spirit that are His bride. It's not every believer that's a bride of Christ. We have a responsibility to make sure we prepare and present ourselves as the bride of Christ. Like the five wise virgins, we must make conscious effort to prepare and present ourselves as the bride of Christ by taking extra oil with us in our lamps. We must consciously and carefully walk with the Holy Spirit of God. Being led by the spirit of God is the hallmark of sonship in the kingdom of our God. That's why Romans 8:14 let us know that "as many as are led by the Spirit of God, these are the sons of God." The ten virgins were supposed to be the bride collectively; unfortunately, the five foolish virgins were not prepared, so only the five wise virgins became the bride collectively. The closing of the wedding door symbolizes the snatching away of the bride of Christ (true church) for the marriage supper of the Lamb in heaven, an event well recorded in Revelation 19:7–9. In short, the Parable of the Ten Virgins is about the marriage supper of the Lamb; that's what the wedding is about. The closing of the wedding door is the snatching away of the church, which is discussed extensively in the next chapter as the vehicle for attending the marriage supper of the Lamb in heaven. If an unprepared believer misses this great "snatching away" event, that person would be left out in the dark when the door has been shut, like the five foolish virgins experienced, to face the Antichrist, the great tribulation, and mark of the beast. God's desire is for all His children to come to heaven for the marriage supper of the Lamb during the great tribulation on earth. God doesn't desire that anyone should be left behind. The foolish virgins did not anticipate that the night would come, and the bridegroom still hasn't arrived. They (the foolish virgins) couldn't learn from this story because they were the casualty of the story in the parable. However, the rest of us reading this right now can learn from the experience of the five foolish virgins so that we do not make the same mistakes as them. We must get prepared for the Lord's soon return. The time is very short. We must get our lamps and vessels filled with fresh oil and trim our lamps so that our light will continue to shine brighter and brighter unto the perfect day (Proverbs 4:18).

## Summary

The Parable of the Ten Virgins has been unveiled in this chapter. The underlying story reveals the ten virgins as being ten believers (Christians). Five were wise, while five were foolish. The lamp symbolizes the word of God, while the oil symbolizes the Holy Spirit. The bridegroom symbolizes the Lord Jesus Christ, and the wedding symbolizes the marriage supper of the Lamb. All ten virgins (believers) are the guests invited to the wedding. The five wise virgins, who successfully made the wedding banquet, are the bride. These five wise virgins had the word of God. They obeyed and yielded to the word of God. They were filled with the Holy Spirit. They honored their bodies as the temple of the Holy Spirit. The wise virgins were Spirit led and had both insight and foresight to do the will of God by taking the extra oil. The five foolish virgins were the opposite of these attributes seen in the wise virgins. They were carnal and walked in the flesh. They were full of darkness and had no light of the Holy Spirit in them. The five wise believers lived their daily Christian lives in anticipation of the Lord's soon return, like a thief at night (Revelation 16:15; Matthew 24:43; and 1 Thessalonians 5:2). They had hope and faith that they would someday hear God's trumpet, announcing the arrival of the bridegroom, as prophetically revealed by the apostle Paul when he declared, "For the Lord Himself will descend from heaven with a shout, with the voice of an archangel, and with the trumpet of God. And the dead in Christ will rise first. Then we who are alive and remain shall be caught up together with them in the clouds to meet the Lord in the air. And thus we shall always be with the Lord" (1 Thessalonians 4:16–17 NKJV). Unfortunately, the five foolish believers were nowhere to be found when the Lord returned to take His bride home for the marriage supper of the Lamb. They were not living daily in anticipation of His return because they were not ready. They were very busy with the affairs of this world, entangling themselves with the things of the world. No wonder the word of God says, "Do not love the world or anything in the world. If anyone loves the world, love for the Father is not in them. For everything in the world—the lust of the flesh, the lust of the eyes, and the pride of life—comes not from the Father but from the world. The world and its desires pass away, but whoever does the will of God lives forever" (1 John 2:15–17).

The five foolish believers loved the world more than they loved the Word. They did not desire to do the will of God. They knew the word of God but were devoid of the Holy Spirit, who gives life to the Word. The Word without the Spirit is mere letter, according to Scriptures:

> Who also hath made us able ministers of the New Testament; not of the letter, but of the spirit: for the letter killeth, but the spirit giveth life. (2 Corinthians 3:6 KJV)

The five foolish believers were acquainted with the letter of the Word and not the Spirit. It is the Spirit that gives life (John 6:63). The life of the Spirit was absent in them. The foolish believers missed the Lord's return. They were left out in outer darkness, where there would be weeping and gnashing of teeth. The Antichrist would unleash his terror on them, with wanton destruction and devastation, during the great tribulation. However, the wise believers have been snatched away for the marriage supper of the Lamb in heaven.

The door is closed against the foolish believers. Here lies a big lesson for every believer reading this today to be ready and not be caught off guard, like the five foolish virgins.

> Watch therefore, for you know neither the day nor the hour in which the Son of Man is coming. (Matthew 25:13 NKJV)

# CHAPTER 6

## Conclusion

As the curtain is drawn on this book, it is pertinent to highlight some of the salient points in the parables that have been unveiled and discussed:

1. *The wisdom of Christ is unfathomable*: The wisdom of Christ has radiated through the parables that have been discussed in this book. One would wonder the unsearchable riches of Christ's wisdom, which was manifested in creating these parables and their hidden messages. It brings to the fore, the fact that Christ is the wisdom of God. He is the wisdom by which God created all things. The good news is, this same wisdom has been given to the one who is in Christ, for Christ has become for us wisdom from God. If you are a believer and you think you are lacking in wisdom, then ask the Lord to give to you according to His word, which says, "If any of you lacks wisdom, you should ask God, who gives generously to all without finding fault, and it will be given to you" (James 1:5).
2. *The Lord Jesus demonstrated that parables have hidden messages*: The Lord Jesus gave more than thirty parables during His earthly ministry; however, only three of these parables were privately explained to His disciples, unveiling the hidden messages in the parables, as discussed in chapter 1. Interestingly,

two out of the three parables unveiled by the Lord pertain to the end-time and the judgment of the world. This underscores the fact that those unveiled parables are for our generation, the end-time generation. There is the urgent need for everyone to be prepared for the soon return of the Lord.

3. *The return of the Gentiles to God's family*: Chapter 2 discussed the Parable of the Prodigal Son, which unveiled God's work of salvation for the return of the Gentiles back to His fold. The righteousness of God in Christ Jesus was seen to be a great gift and a great mystery, setting the foundation upon which every gift and blessing given to the believer in Christ is anchored.

4. *An extravagant wedding feast in heaven*: Chapter 3 unveiled the hidden message in the Parable of the Wedding Feast, where it was found that the wedding feast is the same as the celebration feast in chapter 2, symbolizing the marriage supper of the Lamb. Two key things that were keenly observed in chapter 3 are, first, although everyone is invited to the marriage supper of the Lamb, however, the righteousness of God in Christ Jesus is the basis for being chosen for this wedding. On that day, some will find themselves speechless when they are denied entry to the wedding and be thrown out into outer darkness by the angels of God, even though they were churchgoers, church leaders, and people who lived in the corridors of the church and ministry. These are not enough to qualify anyone for the wedding feast. He that has received the righteousness of Christ must live righteously and be filled with the fruits of righteousness, which are in Jesus Christ (Philippians 1:11). Whoever practices righteousness is righteous (1 John 3:7). Anything to the contrary is unrighteousness to God, and it is not tenable. That was the case with the speechless man in the parable. Second, the wedding bride is a mystery that was hidden throughout the different ages and generations and has been unveiled to be the church of Christ. The church, also known as the body of Christ, are the called-out ones,

*ecclesia* in Greek. The church is a collection of people in whom Christ is alive and indwelling.

5. *The genesis of mankind's problems and the successful execution of God's redemptive plan for all mankind*: Chapter 4 unveiled the hidden message in the Parable of the Good Samaritan, revealing the genesis of mankind's problem, when Adam fell into sin and lost his power and authority and the arrival of the Lord Jesus to save the wounded mankind and to revive him. This led to the birth of the church of Christ, which is both a place and people where the wounded mankind is being revived through the medicines of God's word and the Holy Spirit. In this chapter, it was found that the Lord Jesus set up the church, which is His own body, for a period of two thousand years, with the possibility for added extra time. The church of Christ here on earth is overseen by the Holy Spirit. This chapter further revealed how extremely short the time is before the Lord's return. The two thousand years down payment is nearly exhausted. The remaining time is extremely short, having single-digit years to complete the down payment of two thousand years fixed by the Lord Himself.

6. *The five wise and five foolish believers*: Chapter 5 unveiled the hidden message in the Parable of the Ten Virgins, where it was seen that this is the only parable of the Lord Jesus that pertains exclusively to the church of Christ. It was found in this chapter that the difference between the wise and foolish believers was spiritual insight. While the wise believers were filled with the Holy Spirit and walked closely with the Lord through the help of the Holy Spirit, however, the foolish believers were carnal and were not led by the Spirit; they therefore missed the Master's return. Very importantly, it was also observed in this chapter that the groom's arrival was delayed, therefore corroborating the same point that was earlier made in item 5 above. While all ten believers were seen to know the word of God, however, only the five wise ones were genuinely filled with the Holy

Spirit and walked closely with the Lord. It is the Spirit that gives life to the Word. Without the Spirit, the Word is mere letter, and it kills (2 Corinthians 3:6).

Having done a recap of each chapter and the hidden message unveiled from each parable, the book concludes by sharing further thoughts on the subjects in the four subsections below:

## The marriage supper (wedding feast) of the Lamb

The Lamb's marriage supper or wedding feast featured in three out of four parables that have been unveiled in this book, indicating the significance of this event in God's kingdom. This marriage featured in the Parable of the Prodigal Son in chapter 2, as the celebration feast to welcome the prodigal son back home to his father. The marriage also featured in the Parable of the Wedding Feast in chapter 3, as the wedding feast in the parable. Thirdly, the marriage featured in the Parable of the Ten Virgins in chapter 5, as the marriage that all ten virgins were invited to, but only the five wise virgins successfully made it to the wedding feast, while the five foolish virgins missed it. This marriage is to consummate and celebrate the union between Christ and His bride. It celebrates the return of mankind back to God. This will be a huge feast. You must do everything possible to be chosen to attend this marriage feast. Anyone chosen is surely blessed, according to the scripture, which says, "Then he said to me, 'Write: Blessed are those who are called to the marriage supper of the Lamb!' And he said to me, 'These are the true sayings of God'" (Revelation 19:9 NKJV). This marriage will be the last event in heaven before the Lord Jesus, together with the Old Testament and New Testament saints, returns to earth for the millennial reign of Christ. Everyone that participated in this marriage feast will come with the Lord to earth to reign with Him (Revelation 19:11–14 and Revelation 20:4). This will be an extravagant marriage feast in heaven. The Lord Jesus will be the center of all attention at the wedding feast because He is the groom. The patriarchs of old and all who lived righteously in the Old Testament will be there. The prophets of God throughout the different ages and eras, as well as all righteous kings of Israel that walked faithfully with God, will also be there. The church of Christ is the icing on the cake of God's creation. The church will be gloriously present, together with the Old Testament church. The twenty-four elders will be there, representing the twelve tribes of Israel and the twelve apostles of our Lord Jesus Christ. This wedding feast will bring an end to the church dispensation, as we currently know it, as well as bring about the unification of both the church and the Old Testament saints as one big family of God. This was exactly what happened in the Parable of the Prodigal Son, when the father went to speak with the older son to come and join the celebration party for his lost brother. The older son symbolizes the Old Testament saints, which are only Jews. The younger or prodigal son symbolizes the New Testament church, which contains both Gentiles and Jews but predominantly Gentiles.

At the wedding feast, there will be the coming together of both the Jews and the Gentiles as one big family of God. The Lord Jesus will be the center of all attraction. Angelic music will be provided at the wedding feast by special angels that are divinely, heavenly gifted musicians. On that day, God's people will hear some types of musical tunes that have never been heard anywhere else since creation. The kingdom of God is a lavish and extravagant kingdom. This God that we call our Father in heaven is a very big God. When you pray to God, never limit yourself. Ask Him anything, no matter how big; it cannot be bigger than your Father. This God is a very, very big God. You must let this sink in. Never be beggarly when you pray to God. He is bigger than any requests of yours. I have heard some believers say, "Heaven will be a very boring place as we are going to be like robots in the presence of God." That can never be true. Heaven is a place of joy, peace, and merriment. There is no sorrow, sickness, pain, or death in heaven. We won't be like robots. We will be like the Lord Jesus Christ Himself after His resurrection. We will have glorified, immortal bodies, like the Lord's, bodies not subject to sickness, disease, corruption, depravity, and decadence.

The Lord Jesus purposely stayed back on earth for forty days, following His glorious resurrection, to let us know of this possibility.

During the forty-day period when the Lord was physically present on earth in His glorified, resurrected body, He sat with His disciples, reasoning and discussing important kingdom matters with them (Acts 1:1–9; John 21:10–22; and Matthew 28:16–20). He also ate physical food with them (John 21:10–15; Acts 1:4). He appeared and disappeared from their sight, like He did to the two disciples that met Him on the way to Emmaus (Luke 24:31). He still remembered their names and everything He had been discussing with them, meaning He still had His mind and intellect intact after the resurrection (John 21:15–23; Acts 1:3–9). The Lord could enter a room without the need for a door, like it was when He entered the room where the disciples were gathered and the doors locked (John 20:26). These are some examples of the things that the Lord Jesus did in His glorified, resurrected body. The Lord Jesus is our example and model. This is exactly the way the saints of God will be in their glorified bodies in heaven and when they return with the Lord to earth for the millennial reign of Christ.

The Christian is like Christ. That is the reason why he is called a Christian, which means "like Christ." The Christian does not look like an angel or the patriarchs; the Christian looks like Christ. This is why 1 John 3:2 says, "But we know that when Christ appears, we shall be like him." We shall be like the Lord when we see Him. For as He is, so are we in this world (1 John 4:17). In heaven, the saints of God won't look like robots; we will all look like our Lord and Savior, Jesus Christ. When we get to heaven, you will confirm this. Nevertheless, we should pray to get there first. That is the first and most important thing. The Lord Jesus is waiting for this wedding feast to drink the communion cup with us in person. On *that day*, we will have communion with the Lord Jesus. The Lord confirmed this Himself at the communion table with His disciples when He said, "I tell you, I will not drink from this fruit of the vine from now on until *that day* when I drink it new with you in my Father's kingdom" (Matthew 26:29). The italicized phrase "that day" refers to the day of the wedding feast.

Immediately after the Lamb's wedding feast, the Lamb, the Lord Jesus Christ, will get ready for war as a warrior. He will be dressed in a robe dipped in blood, which signifies the blood that He shed on the cross for the salvation of mankind. This blood gives Him the legal right to stand as the judge of all mankind. He paid in full to ransom mankind. He will ride on a white horse, along with the saints (comprising of both the Old and New Testament saints), to establish His millennial reign on earth, in what is commonly known as the second coming of Christ. The Lord Jesus Christ will defeat the beast (the Antichrist) and his army. The wedding feast precedes this war, as clearly expressed by the Spirit of God, through the apostle John in Revelation 19 when the following verses are read together as one:

> "Let us rejoice and be glad and give him glory! For the wedding of the Lamb has come, and his bride has made herself ready. Fine linen, bright and clean, was given her to wear." (Fine linen stands for the righteous acts of God's holy people.) Then the angel said to me, "Write this: Blessed are those who are invited to the wedding supper of the Lamb!" And he added, "These are the true words of God." I saw heaven standing open and there before me was a white horse, whose rider is called Faithful and True. With justice he judges and wages war. His eyes are like blazing fire, and on his head are many crowns. He has a name written on him that no one knows but he himself. He is dressed in a robe dipped in blood, and his name is the Word of God. The armies of heaven were following him, riding on white horses and dressed in fine linen, white and clean. Coming out of his mouth is a sharp sword with which to strike down the nations. "He will rule them with an iron scepter." He treads the winepress of the fury of the wrath of God Almighty. On his robe and on his thigh he has this name written: king of kings and Lord of Lords. And I saw an angel standing in the sun,

> who cried in a loud voice to all the birds flying in midair, "Come, gather together for the great supper of God, so that you may eat the flesh of kings, generals, and the mighty, of horses and their riders, and the flesh of all people, free and slave, great and small." Then I saw the beast and the kings of the earth and their armies gathered together to wage war against the rider on the horse and his army. But the beast was captured, and with it the false prophet who had performed the signs on its behalf. With these signs he had deluded those who had received the mark of the beast and worshiped its image. The two of them were thrown alive into the fiery lake of burning sulfur. The rest were killed with the sword coming out of the mouth of the rider on the horse, and all the birds gorged themselves on their flesh. (Revelation 19:7–9, 11–21)

The quoted verses above in Revelation 19 contain two different events that occurred successively: the Lamb's wedding feast in heaven, followed by the war and defeat of the beast and his army on earth. These two events are the same as the two events prophetically given by the sons of Korah, by the same spirit of God, in Psalm 45, saying:

> My heart is stirred by a noble theme as I recite my verses for the king; my tongue is the pen of a skillful writer. You are the most excellent of men and your lips have been anointed with grace, since God has blessed you forever. Gird your sword on your side, you mighty one; clothe yourself with splendor and majesty. In your majesty ride forth victoriously in the cause of truth, humility and justice; let your right hand achieve awesome deeds. Let your sharp arrows pierce

the hearts of the king's enemies; let the nations fall beneath your feet. Your throne, O God, will last for ever and ever; a scepter of justice will be the scepter of your kingdom. You love righteousness and hate wickedness; therefore God, your God, has set you above your companions by anointing you with the oil of joy. All your robes are fragrant with myrrh and aloes and cassia; from palaces adorned with ivory the music of the strings makes you glad. Daughters of kings are among your honored women; at your right hand is the royal bride in gold of Ophir. Listen, daughter, and pay careful attention: Forget your people and your father's house. Let the king be enthralled by your beauty; honor him, for he is your Lord. The city of Tyre will come with a gift, people of wealth will seek your favor. All glorious is the princess within her chamber; her gown is interwoven with gold. In embroidered garments she is led to the king; her virgin companions follow her— those brought to be with her. Led in with joy and gladness, they enter the palace of the king. Your sons will take the place of your fathers; you will make them princes throughout the land. I will perpetuate your memory through all generations; therefore the nations will praise you for ever and ever. (Psalm 45:1–17)

The spirit of God unveiled this same revelation to the sons of Korah more than one thousand years before Christ was born. This shows the significance of this event. Psalm 45 has to do with the Lamb's wedding feast and the war against His enemies. Both Revelation 19 and Psalm 45 are prophetically one and the same scripture, although rendered in different ways. The King in Psalm 45 is the same as the Lamb in Revelation 19. The royal bride at His right hand is the same as the bride in Revelation 19. The King's enemy is the same as the

Antichrist that was defeated in Revelation 19. Both Revelation 19 and Psalm 45 are one and the same event of Scripture, even though they are more than one thousand years apart in terms of the difference in the time between both prophetic revelations. The two main events contained in both passages are transitional events. The Lamb's wedding feast brings an end to the church age, unifying both the Old and New Testament saints as one people of God. The war against the beast and his army heralds the beginning of a new age, which ushers in the millennial reign of the Lord Jesus Christ here on earth. This is why these two events captured in these two different passages of Scripture are so significant. They are transitional events. One brings an end to one age, while the other heralds the start of another age, a glorious age when God Himself will be physically present on earth as the King of the whole world. He will rule the earth with justice and righteousness (Isaiah 9:7). The earth will experience its greatest era of peace, joy, prosperity, and righteousness. Hallelujah!

## The vehicle for attending the marriage supper of the Lamb in heaven

The Lord will provide transport to everyone that is chosen to come to heaven for the marriage supper of the Lamb. The transport is by means of a flight that will take off suddenly from earth in the twinkling of an eye. This is what the Bible says about this flight:

> For the Lord Himself will come down from heaven with a shout of command, with the voice of the archangel and with the [blast of the] trumpet of God, and the dead in Christ will rise first. Then we who are alive and remain [on the earth] will simultaneously be *caught up (raptured)* together with them [the resurrected ones] in the clouds to meet the Lord in the air, and so we will always be with the Lord! (1 Thessalonians 4:16–17 AMP)

The phrase "caught up" is from the Greek word *harpazo*, which means the same thing as the Latin word *rapturo*. Both words mean "to snatch away" or "to take away." The Latin word *rapturo* is anglicized as the word *rapture* in English. The rapture, which is found in 1 Thessalonians 4:16–17, is the vehicle that will be used to transport those on earth that are chosen for the marriage supper of the Lamb in heaven. Those that died in Christ will be transported first, and then followed simultaneously by those who are in Christ and are alive at the time. The rapture of the church is not widely covered in the Bible because it is a great mystery of God, carefully hidden in the word of God, as expressed by the apostle Paul when he said, "Take notice! I tell you a mystery (a secret truth, an event decreed by the hidden purpose or counsel of God). We shall not all fall asleep [in death], but we shall all be changed (transformed). *In a moment, in the twinkling of an eye*, at the [sound of the] last trumpet call. For a trumpet will sound, and the dead [in Christ] will be raised imperishable (free and immune from decay), and we shall be changed (transformed)" (2 Corinthians 15:51–52 AMPC). The rapture will happen in a moment, in the twinkling of an eye. It is going to happen suddenly. You must prepare for it beforehand. You can't prepare for it on the day of the event; it will be too late by then.

The rapture of the church is not a matter of scriptural doctrine or principle; it is a scriptural mystery. Mysteries are only understood through the help of the Holy Spirit and the insights He provides. The former scripture in 1 Thessalonians 4:16–17 and the latter one in 2 Corinthians 15:51–52 both refer to the same thing: the rapture. Both scriptures are one and the same, rendered in different ways. The contexts and the meanings of both scriptures remain the same. The Living Bible rendering of the latter scripture simplifies it for ease of understanding:

> But I am telling you this strange and wonderful secret: we shall not all die, but we shall all be given new bodies! It will all happen in a moment, in the twinkling of an eye, when the last trumpet is blown. For there will be a trum-

> pet blast from the sky, and all the Christians who have died will suddenly become alive, with new bodies that will never, never die; and then we who are still alive shall suddenly have new bodies too. For our earthly bodies, the ones we have now that can die, must be transformed into heavenly bodies that cannot perish but will live forever. (2 Corinthians 15:51–53 TLB)

The rapture is a strange and wonderful secret. It is a secret truth decreed by the hidden purpose or counsel of God. The rapture will happen at least seven years before the Lord Jesus returns for His millennial reign on earth. While the church is in heaven for the marriage supper of the Lamb, the devil will take advantage of the church's absence to return to earth, through the Antichrist, to torment the earth and its inhabitants in what is known as the great tribulation. This will be a period of severe darkness upon the earth. Remember, the church is the light of the world (Matthew 5:16). The Lord Jesus, the head of the church, said, "As long as I am in the world, I am the light of the world" (John 9:5 KJV). Like the Lord Jesus, as long as the church is in the world, the church is the light of the world. Once the church is suddenly taken away to heaven, the light of the world would be gone. That would herald an era of great darkness upon the earth and its inhabitants, ushering in the great tribulation, a time when evil and mayhem will reign supreme on earth, unhindered. This tribulation would be so terrible that, according to the words of the Lord Jesus, if those days are not shortened, no flesh would be saved.

> For then there will be great tribulation, such as has not been since the beginning of the world until this time, no, nor ever shall be. And unless those days were shortened, no flesh would be saved; but for the elect's sake those days will be shortened. (Matthew 24:21–22 NKJV)

Thankfully, the time will be shortened, from seven years to three and half years, for the sake of the Jews, God's elected ones. The church will already be gone to heaven in the rapture before this time, so the Jewish people, those who have not received the gospel of Christ, will be here to face the great tribulation, along with the rest of the ungodly. But because our God is a God of mercy and compassion, He will have mercy on Israel because of His eternal covenant with father Abraham. Therefore, God will shorten the tribulation time for Israel's sake, as well as cause the earth to help and shield the people of Israel from the Antichrist, the evil one. All of these are recorded in Scripture in the book of Daniel. They are also found in the book of Revelation, particularly Revelation 12:1–17. God will provide divine help for Israel during the great tribulation, as recorded in Revelation 12:15–16:

> Then from his mouth the serpent spewed water like a river, to overtake the woman and sweep her away with the torrent. *But the earth helped the woman* by opening its mouth and swallowing the river that the dragon had spewed out of his mouth.

The woman in this scripture symbolizes Israel, the mother nation of Christ and His church, which is His body. The serpent is the Antichrist, the devil. During the great tribulation, the Antichrist will severely persecute the children of Israel, which is symbolized by the spewing of water. (The water means trouble and tribulation.) God, in His eternal mercy and faithfulness, will send nations of the earth to provide help for the Jews. God loves the children of Israel. Although they have rejected Christ as a nation, but God has not abandoned them. Remember, in the Parable of the Prodigal Son in chapter 2, we found that Israel is God's first son. God will not abandon His first son. He wants him to repent and turn to Him by accepting His one and only begotten Son, Jesus Christ. Until the church of Christ is taken away to heaven in the rapture, the Antichrist cannot be revealed, let alone begin the great tribulation. The church is the light of the world, while the Antichrist represents the kingdom of darkness. It is not possible for both light and darkness to coexist. Therefore, it is not possible for the great tribulation, a period of absolute reign of the devil and his agents here on earth, to happen when the church is still here on earth. If light and darkness are together, there is only one outcome: the light will overcome and obliterate the darkness. This is what the Bible says:

> The light shines in the darkness, and the darkness can never extinguish it. (John 1:5 NLT)

The apostle Paul, by the spirit of God, let us know that the church must be taken away first before the Antichrist can be revealed on earth:

> For the secret power of lawlessness is already at work; but the one who now holds it back will continue to do so till *he is taken out of the way*. And then the lawless one will be revealed, whom the Lord Jesus will overthrow with the breath of his mouth and destroy by the splendor of his coming. (2 Thessalonians 2:7–8)

The church of Christ is currently the one holding back the devil from taking full control of the earth to unleash his terror and mayhem. Once the church is taken out of the way, as expressed in this scripture, then the Antichrist will be fully revealed to unleash the great tribulation on the inhabitants of the earth. The "taken out of the way" of the church is the same as the rapture. Some say it is the Holy Spirit that will be taken out of the way, not the church. My answer to such suggestion is, why is the Holy Spirit on earth in the first place? Isn't He here because of the church? The Holy Spirit is the Comforter and helper of the church. He is the overseer of God's church on earth. The Lord Jesus promised to send us the Holy Spirit, who will be with us forever, not for a season and then go away. No, He will be with the church forever. That means, if the Holy Spirit were to be taken away, He will take the church along with Him to heaven. The Lord Jesus says, "And I will ask the Father, and he will give you another advocate to help you and be with you forever—the Spirit of truth. The world cannot accept him, because it neither sees him nor knows him. But you know him, for he lives with you and will be in you" (John 16:16–17). From this scripture, it is obvious that the Holy Spirit is given for the church, not for the world. The world cannot accept or see or know Him. Until and unless a man repents and receives Christ, that man can never receive the Holy Spirit of God.

Recall the Salvation Flow Chart earlier in figure 1. A man must first repent before receiving righteousness (the best robe) and then the Holy Spirit (the ring). The world cannot receive the ring until they have first received the best robe. Therefore, the Holy Spirit is only available to those who have repented and received the righteousness of God, which is by faith in Christ Jesus, and that is the church or body of Christ. A man cannot receive the Holy Spirit unless He is first born again. Since the Holy Spirit is not with the world but with the church, therefore, if for any reason He is to be taken away from the earth, the church must go with Him. The Lord Jesus has already assured us that the Holy Spirit will be with the church forever; therefore anywhere the Holy Spirit goes, the church goes with Him. Recall the Parable of the Good Samaritan in chapter 4, where the innkeeper symbolizes the Holy Spirit, and the inn symbolizes the church. It is clearly impossible for the innkeeper to abandon the wounded man he is reviving in the inn. If he does so, the thieves that attacked him earlier and put him in that state would show up again to finish him off and undo all the work of revival that the innkeeper has been doing over the last two thousand years. That would make no sense at all. That is exactly what it would mean if the Holy Spirit were to be taken away from the earth, while the church is left out in the dark to face the great tribulation all by itself. Without the Holy Spirit, the One carrying the *dunamis* power of God, the church would be powerless and weak, leaving her at the mercy of the Antichrist. The devil is merciless and has no capacity to show mercy. He would easily destroy and overrun the church of Christ if left without the Holy

Spirit. So this possibility is nonexistent. Without the Holy Spirit, the church of Christ would not exist. The Holy Spirit is the reason why the church belongs to Christ. Without Him, there will be no Church. This is why Romans 8:9 says, "And if anyone does not have the spirit of Christ, they do not belong to Christ."

Having explained this, it is therefore obvious that the one to be taken out of the way before the Antichrist can be revealed on earth is the church of Jesus Christ, and that taken away or being snatched away is what is popularly referred to as the rapture. This rapture is the vehicle that the church will use to get to heaven for the marriage supper of the Lamb. If a believer is not prepared and misses the rapture, that believer would have to go through the ugly darkness and sorrow of the great tribulation, which would expose that believer to the risk of being forced to take the mark of the beast (Revelation 13:16–17); everyone that takes that mark would be eternally condemned (Revelation 14:9–11). If anyone takes the mark of the beast, redemption will expire for that individual. They would become irredeemable, facing the full wrath and indignation of God, where they would be tormented with fire and brimstone.

> Then a third angel followed them, saying with a loud voice, "If anyone worships the beast and his image, and receives his mark on his forehead or on his hand, he himself shall also drink of the wine of the wrath of God, which is poured out full strength into the cup of His indignation. He shall be tormented with fire and brimstone in the presence of the holy angels and in the presence of the Lamb. And the smoke of their torment ascends forever and ever; and they have no rest day or night, who worship the beast and his image, and whoever receives the mark of his name." (Revelation 14:9–11)

This is why the Lord wants us to be prepared and not miss the rapture. The Antichrist will hold sway on earth for seven years, but the first half of this period (three and half years or forty-two months) will be relatively peaceful, while the second half will be brutal and utterly wicked (Revelation 13:1–9). Daniel, by the spirit of God, prophesied this, saying, "This king will make a seven-year treaty with the people, but after half that time, he will break his pledge and stop the Jews from all their sacrifices and their offerings; then, as a climax to all his terrible deeds, the Enemy shall utterly defile the sanctuary of God. But in God's time and plan, his judgment will be poured out upon this Evil One" (Daniel 9:27 TLB). An unprepared believer who missed the rapture would have to go through the great tribulation to face the Antichrist, with the strong possibility of being forced to take the mark of the beast, which would lead to eternal condemnation. That was the case with the five foolish virgins, which are five carnal believers that did not live by the Spirit. They were not prepared for the rapture; as a result, they were left behind and the door of the rapture was shut against them. We must all learn from the lesson of the five foolish virgins so that we too don't make the same mistakes they made. We should emulate the five wise virgins and live righteously for the Lord, living and walking in the Spirit. This is why the Parable of the Ten Virgins concludes with the warning:

> Watch therefore, for you know neither the day nor the hour in which the Son of Man is coming. (Matthew 25:13 NKJV)

The time is very short. The rapture of the church is around the corner and even at the door. Everyone must be watchful and prepared.

> So you also must be ready, because the Son of Man will come at an hour when you do not expect him. (Matthew 24:44)

> He who has an ear, let him hear what the Spirit says to the churches. (Revelation 2:29 NKJV)

## Always keep your best robe clean

The divine life of Christ in us must be kept clean always through the living word of God. The word of God is the food for this divine life. That is the reason why the Lord Jesus said, "Man shall not live on bread alone, but on every word that comes from the mouth of God" (Matthew 4:4). The believer must therefore continue to feed daily on the word of God. The best robe is kept always clean through the word of God, as also corroborated by the psalmist when he said, "How can a young person stay on the path of purity? By living according to your word. I have hidden your word in my heart that I might not sin against you" (Psalm 119:9, 11). The believer would remain on the path of purity by living according to the word of God.

The word of God in the heart of the believer is the antidote to sin. When the heart is saturated with the holy word of God and the Holy Spirit, sin would find no inroads into that life. This life of the kingdom is lived by faith, and it is the word of God that brings faith, according to scripture, which says, "So then faith comes by hearing, and hearing by the word of God" (Romans 10:17 NKJV). The faith to successfully live the divine life on earth comes from the word of God and the Holy Spirit. This is why it is imperative that the believer must continue to feed his divine life with fresh supply of the word of God. Having been justified by faith, according to Romans 5:1, the believer also requires faith to continue to live this life of justification or righteousness. This is the reason why the word of God says, "But the righteous will live by his faith [in the true God]" (Habakkuk 2:4 AMP). To demonstrate the importance of living the righteous life by faith, the scripture in Habakkuk 2:4 has been repeated three times in the New Testament as a matter of emphasis (Romans 1:17; Galatians 3:11; and Hebrews 10:38). The life of faith is not optional but mandatory for the believer. Without faith, the believer cannot please God (Hebrews 11:6). Therefore, to live this divine life in Christ Jesus to the full, successfully and effectively, we must build our faith through the word of the living God and live by faith always. Enoch was the first man to be taken away from the earth alive, without seeing death (Genesis 5:24). He was taken away means he was raptured from the earth to heaven. Enoch was the first man on earth to be raptured to heaven, and the word of God tells us that Enoch was a man that had faith and pleased God. We, too, as we wait upon the Lord for the rapture of the church, must continue to live by faith while pleasing God all the time:

> By faith Enoch was taken from this life, so that he did not experience death: 'He could not be found, because God had taken him away.' For before he was taken, he was commended as one who pleased God. And without faith it is impossible to please God, because anyone who comes to him must believe that he exists and that he rewards those who earnestly seek him. (Hebrews 11:5–6)

Wash your robe daily with the living water of God's word. The word of God is the water by which a man gets born-again (John 3:5). The same Word is the water by which the bride of Christ (church) is continuously cleansed and washed so that she can remain holy, pure, blameless, radiant, without stain, or wrinkle before the bridegroom.

> To make her holy, cleansing her by the washing with water through the word, and to present her to himself as a radiant church, without stain or wrinkle or any other blemish, but holy and blameless. (Ephesians 5:26–27)

According to the words of our Lord Jesus Christ, you are blessed if you keep your robe washed; it gives you the right to the tree of life.

> Blessed are those who wash their robes, that they may have the right to the tree of life and may go through the gates into the city. (Revelation 22:14)

## The extraordinary compassion of God

The extraordinary compassion of God for mankind is visibly manifested in two of the parables discussed in this book. The compassion and mercy of God for mankind is unfathomable. The first is seen in the Parable of the Prodigal Son in chapter 2, where we saw the extraordinary compassion of God for the Gentiles, bringing them into the family of God and reconnecting them with the blessing of Abraham. God is full of love, mercy, and compassion, and that was abundantly manifested in bringing back the Gentiles to Himself. Second, in the Parable of the Good Samaritan, we saw the deep love, mercy, and extraordinary compassion of the Lord Jesus Christ toward the wounded mankind. We also saw the innkeeper, symbolizing the Holy Spirit, nursing and looking after this wounded mankind in the inn. So God the Father had compassion, God the Son had compassion, and God the Holy Spirit also showed compassion by taking care of the wounded man. No wonder the Bible says, "When Jesus landed and saw a large crowd, he had compassion on them and healed their sick" (Matthew 14:14).

The Lord Jesus is full of compassion. He is always moved with compassion for mankind. He went about doing good and healing everyone that was oppressed by the devil:

> How God anointed Jesus of Nazareth with the Holy Spirit and with power, who went about doing good and healing all who were oppressed by the devil, for God was with Him. (Acts 10:38)

He even went beyond doing good to paying the ultimate price for the salvation of mankind. While we were yet sinners, Christ died for us.

> Greater love has no one than this: to lay down one's life for one's friends. (John 15:13)

In demonstration of His love and compassion for mankind, He laid His life and paid the ultimate price to procure the salvation of humankind. How do you respond to this great compassion of Christ? The Bible says, "For God so loved the world that he gave his one and only Son, that whoever believes in him shall not perish but have eternal life" (John 3:16). God gave His Son, Jesus, to die for you and me. The Lord Jesus was born to die. He died for you and me. How would you respond to this display of extraordinary love and compassion? If you are reading this, and you have not yet received the Lord Jesus Christ into your life, this is your opportunity to do so. This is your moment. May I kindly invite you to pray the following salvation prayer and mean it from the depth of your heart:

> Dear Lord Jesus Christ, I repent of my sins, and I receive You into my heart today. I believe that You are the Son of the living God. I believe that You died for my sins, and God raised You back to life. I believe that You are alive today and forevermore. I confess with my mouth that You are the Lord and Savior of my life from today. Through Your holy name, Jesus Christ, I'm justified. I'm now the righteousness of God in Christ Jesus. I have eternal life. I'm born again and on my way to heaven. Thank You, Lord. Please fill me with Your precious Holy Spirit and write my name in the Book of Life in the name of Jesus Christ. Amen.

Congratulations! You are now born again and a child of God. Welcome to the family of God Almighty. May the Lord richly bless you and keep you. May the Lord fill you with His precious Holy Spirit in the name of Jesus Christ. Amen!

# ABOUT THE AUTHOR

Dr. Festus Agbonzikilo is a British-Nigerian teacher and preacher of God's word—an anointed prophetic scribe whose ministry encompasses teaching, preaching, the prophetic, evangelism, and discipleship. He is a British chartered mechanical engineer and holds a PhD in mechanical engineering from the University of Lincoln–England. He also holds a master's degree in thermal power engineering from Cranfield University–England and a bachelor's degree in mechanical engineering from the University of Benin–Nigeria. He has authored several scientific and technical publications in the global field of engineering and technology. He is happily married to his sweetheart, Esther, and blessed with two beautiful daughters, Godsblessing and Godsgoodness.

Printed in the USA
CPSIA information can be obtained
at www.ICGtesting.com
CBHW030251081024
15373CB00046BB/946

9 798893 451696